Shadows

by

Fr. Jimmy Collins

Published by
O'Reagan Publications Ltd
Warrington

Shadows

Published in 2005

O'Reagan Publications Ltd.
5. Friars Ave. Great Sankey. Warrington. WA5 2AR

ISBN. 0-9551754-0-2
ISBN. 978-0-9551754-0-4

Printed in the U.K
by
Gemini Print (Wigan) Ltd
Unit A, Redgate Road, South Lancs Industrial Estate,
Bryn, Nr. Wigan. WN4 8DT
Tel: 01942 712480

Contents

PSALM 138

Hymn of thanksgiving

I thank you, Yahweh, with all my heart,
because you have heard what I said.
In the presence of the angels I pray for you,
and bow down towards your holy Temple.

I give thanks to your name for your love and faithfulness,
your promise is even greater than your fame.
The day I called for help, you heard me
and you increased my strength.

Yahweh, all kings on earth give thanks to you,
for they have heard your promises,
they celebrate Yahweh's actions,
Great is the glory of Yahweh!'
From far above, Yahweh sees the humble,
from far away he marks down the arrogant.

Though I live surrounded by trouble,
you keep me alive—to my enemies' fury!
You stretch your hand out and save me,
your right hand will do everything for me.
Yahweh, your love is everlasting,
do not abandon us whom you have made.

Fr. Jimmy Collins

Fr Jimmy Collins is a retired Catholic priest who served for 55 years in the Archdiocese of Liverpool, the city in which he was born; first as a curate in a number of parishes and then parish priest in one of the most densely populated and deprived areas in the country.

His compilation of spiritual essays of parish life and personal experiences are unique; they reflect the joys, heartaches and warmth of the people he loves. In a special way he brings his holy priesthood to life by the complete sharing of his vocation, always with God at the centre.

After his retirement in 1996, Fr Jimmy in thanksgiving for his holy priesthood, walked 220 miles on pilgrimage, from Wigan in the Northwest of England to Walsingham, *(England's national Shrine to The Blessed Virgin)* in Norfolk. It was to be a pilgrimage of thanksgiving. He is five foot two inches in height, weighs less than seven stone, and was seventy-eight years old.

Currently he has given himself tirelessly to the Healing Ministry, as well as giving endless retreats.

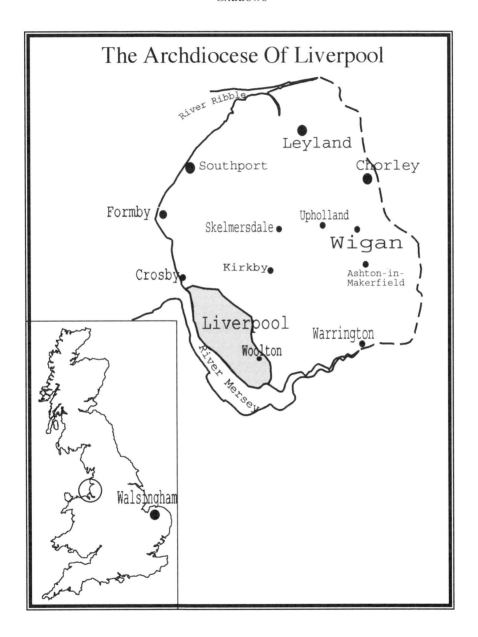

The Archdiocese Of Liverpool

Also in this series of short stories
by Fr Jimmy Collins:

A Bird Sings In The Winter.

She Smiled At Me.

Reflections.

Wild Flowers In The Moorland.

Soft Blows The Wind.
(The story of his pilgrimage to Walsingham.)

1

The Decision

ᘓᘔᘓᘔᘓᘔᘓᘔᘓᘔ

There was a woman in the parish who had four children, all young, the oldest being eight and there was some genetic defect in either the husband or herself. In that era I was shy about asking questions, which were very personal, so I did not ask which of the pair had the problem. But it was a serious one.

Three of the children had been affected by it, all three would die before the age of ten. So said the consultants, and so it turned out to be. There were three funerals. Three little coffins in consecutive years, with just the twelve months in between for mourning each one in turn. The husband never talked to me when I called. He was affable but silent, he would excuse himself and go to work on some wooden construction he had begun in the garden shed. The woman of the house did the talking and the weeping. Her hair went white and she offered it a different colour which the hair gratefully accepted, and kept her looking tolerably young.

She had been a devout Catholic, but after the letter by Paul V1 about contraception, she stopped receiving Holy Communion, and it had me wondering a lot about that particular letter by the Pope, but I was the parish priest, the official bearer of the Good News, even when it was bad news, so I said nothing.

We, the priests, we all clammed up and watched people like that woman drift away, and they did, in hundreds, leaving a lot of empty seats in the church. In fact we stopped talking about sexuality in any shape or form, because the kids anyway rejected the traditional stuff scornfully, and got all their information from the girly magazines and the other papers their older brothers or sisters bought from under the counter of the local shop. In any case that woman I knew was one of the victims of the culture and I did not see her for some time.

But one day she came back to me and said, "I'm pregnant." I guessed that something had gone wrong with whatever she was depending on. I knew from the agony in her thin face that her conscience was presenting something to her mind that she did not want to think about, but could not escape: she had to make decisions. "Have you had a scan?" I asked, pretending I knew more about it than I did. She nodded. "The scan tells me nothing" she said. "They want to take a blood test and other tests. That will give me more information." "Please let me know" I said. I called to the house a week later. "Is there any news?" I asked. The surviving girl had started school and the husband was at work. She nodded, and avoided my eyes. "They say the chances that the baby will be normal are very slight." She paused and there was a silence in the room so intense that I could hear a bird singing on a tree somewhere in the distance. "We can pray," I said "for prayer changes everything."

"Doctors are limited in their knowledge; God talks a different language." She listened to this, but I felt that she was not convinced. I knew what advice they had given her, and she knew that I knew. We never mentioned the word termination and avoided the phrase 'have an abortion.' Again the long silence, she began to weep. "I cannot face another funeral after looking at the face and feeling the arms and the growing love of my child. I couldn't bear to see the child smiling at me, tugging at me, and know I would bury it within twelve months."

She was sitting at the table in the kitchen. I sat opposite her. I could not bear to say anything more because I was dealing with a dimension which doctrine could not solve. I began to say the Hail Mary slowly aloud, then another, and another. She joined in the end of it "Holy Mary, Mother of God, pray for us sinners." It was all she said, but it seemed to calm her, a mother appealing to a woman who was a mother, as though she would understand and God might not. She was on my mind constantly.

I offered Mass for her and offered up everything to God, which, I felt could help. So, some eight weeks passed and I knew it was time for me to go back to see her. The street in which she lived was on the edge of the parish. The windows of the house were blank, a "For Sale" notice swung on a board in the autumn wind. I never knew for certain why they had fled, or whether the empty house was a symbol.

2

Our Hospitals Have Realised A Christian Dream.
సారాసారాసారాసారా

There were four beds in the room, which was spacious, white and clinical, and high up on the ninth floor of the hospital.

One young man and two elderly gentlemen were to be my companions. We introduce ourselves but then drift into that interior world where we speculate about ourselves and the others without communicating anything.

Men are not as chatty as women. They hide behind the newspapers, the Mirror, the Echo, reading garbage because there is nothing else to do. The nurse comes in; she is young, probably from India. Indian nurses are always quiet. She wheels a machine from a corner of the room, wraps a large piece of rubber around the upper part of my arm and reads blood pressures on the dial of the machine. She picks up a cardboard folder from the end of the bed, makes notes, puts it back in its place and says nothing. She goes out like a ghost.

My mind is racing. I assume the older men are married, possibly widowed. One of them has two 'get well' cards on the top of his locker, the other has none. I will wait and see when the visitors come. With the young man there is a young lady sitting close to the bed. I guess they will be weighing me up, as well. They will know I am something religious by the cut of my clothes and the breviary on the locker by my side. Later the rosary is put on top of the breviary.

I go across the room and talk with them. It is inconsequential talk, about how long is the stay in the hospital, news about football, and about the weather.

Two nurses come in with a lot of clatter. They are Scousers, brimful of humour and noise. Trolleys rattle across the floor; a blonde tea lady dishes out the drinks. "Milk and sugar, love?" I nod. She is followed by the doctors, the anaesthetists who look grimly at me as though reckoning how much of the stuff will put me out.

Visitors drift in and out. A lad comes in shouting, "Echo," and collects his money. They tell me "nothing to eat and drink after midnight," and put a long needle in my vein with a tap on the top to receive the 'drip.'

Gales of laughter drift along the corridor from the nurses' station. The night staff have arrived. I drift into sleep. I wake before dawn. Two of the night staff are men. One is a tall dignified African, like a Massai warrior. The other looks so much one of the characters from the TV series 'Casualty.' They hurry me into a shower, a surgical gown to cover me. People in uniforms roll my bed out of the ward and down the long corridor. The surgical theatres are upstairs, so we go into a lift and then into an area buzzing with men and women dressed in green. They are all very cheerful.

I lie in the bed like a mackerel caught in a net. The high priests of the theatre gather around me and I go into a world of darkness. Is it day or night? Is it Friday or Saturday? I drift through a long period of hallucination and spectres floating away out of sight. I am thirsty but cannot drink, dimly feel pain but go into blackness.

I become aware of nurses, male and female, looking after me, and it is comforting, and then suddenly it is daylight and the cheerful male nurse gives me a cup of tea. Life has started again.

The breakfast trolley rolls in. "Sugar in your tea, love, toast and marmalade?" The tall blonde is back, twenty-four hours later it is Sunday. I ask the nurse if there is a chapel in the hospital. She was unsure, but her companion says yes, it is lower down. I ask the time of Mass. They don't know. Nor, apparently, does anyone else. They phone to Information and come back with the answer.

The Mass will be at four o'clock. Soon afterwards a Eucharistic Minister comes to see me. It was so good to see her and we talk.

In the months which passed since I had the privilege of being a hospital chaplain, the rules have changed. It means one has to state clearly that one would like to see the chaplain and do it at the time of admission.

Is there a danger that people will die without the Last Sacraments because some bureaucrat has made this rule? These great modern hospitals of our country, which take care of the rich, the poor, the destitute and the abandoned with such care, quality and efficiency are the realisation of the Christian dream. We must not allow them to be turned from their path.

3

In Search Of Telling Signs Within Our Festive Season.

∽⧸∽⧸∽⧸∽⧸∽⧸∽⧸

I was sitting in the lounge of a large house built in the time of Queen Victoria.

Outside, a grey mist was swirling around the stone buildings in the Yorkshire Street. The windows down the long road were illumined by festive lights and the occasional Christmas tree with its own festoon of coloured lights.

It was Christmas Day 2002, early afternoon. Piled up beside me was a large heap of toys. There were trucks which trundled around the floor at the command of a zapper, wagons, builders' hats to fit a three year old, endless dolls, teddies, fluffy bears, cats, dogs, squirrels, rabbits, toy work-benches, with hammers, saws, chisels, books, videos of monsters and other colourful characters, tea sets, dolls houses, and the odd space suit to fit a four year old.

I could not imagine Santa bringing all these down the large Victorian chimney in one night. I guessed some might be left over from some other festive occasion such as a birthday. But, meanwhile, the centre of the floor was a whirl of activity as five young children fought for and unwrapped the latest batch, which had, I gather, arrived during the night.

The remains of Christmas wrapping was everywhere and a boy, not yet three years old, was declaring loudly that "this is mine," as he fought off an older sister and a younger cousin, while his mother was pleading to them all that they must share. But sharing was not on their agenda. Not yet anyway. It is too early.

I have deep misgivings about how we handle the Christmas present business; something has gone wrong.

Later, I talked with the father of the young boys. They were older than the first group but not yet far advanced into adolescence. They had presents like Play Stations or new computer software. They disappeared with their separate computers or televisions. So neither Santa Claus nor Mr Mike Rowsoft appeared keen on building communities.

It did not look to me like a fulfilment of the prophecy of Isaiah which we read at Christmas: 'The wolf shall dwell with the lamb, and the leopard shall lie down with the kid, the calf and the fatling together, a little child shall lead them."

I ponder a good deal about these simple facts of our world because it is so often in the little things that the Spirit is speaking to us and we have to "read the signs of the times," as Jesus said.

The question arises, how do we use our fleeting affluence in such a way that we do not ruin childhood? For one of the great insights of the last decade is the need to safeguard the child. That means a lot more than saving the children from sexual or physical abuse. The saucer of cream can kill the cat. This was also highlighted for me by a conversation I had with my relative before leaving her hospitable home.

She talked about her Muslim neighbours and told me that at the end of Ramadan the mother and children bring her dishes of rice specially cooked in the manner of their culture. For it is the law of the big fasting period that they seek out the widow, the orphan and the poor to share their food with them.

They come down the street, with the food in covered dishes and, smiling, offer it. Apparently this is done before they eat the food themselves. What is significant also is that it is preceded by fasting, not by shopping and celebration parties in clubs and restaurants.

I know this is cold comfort following our Merry Christmas Season but it has to be looked at because it squares with something I heard old people talk about in Kirkby. It was that, in the squalid slums in which so many of them began, they always shared what they had with poorer families. And what they had was very little.

This phenomenon is also seen in countries whose people live well below the poverty line. I understand that this is unpopular. Charles Dickens was unpopular in the 1850's when, after seeing the lives of the poor workers he wrote, 'A Christmas Carol.' Christmas does tempt us into excess and it can cast a cloud over our feast.

4

Tolerance Is Charity. So Blessed Be The Tolerant.
≼᠗ᠵ᠗ᠵ᠗ᠵ᠗ᠵ᠗ᠵ᠗ᠵ᠗

Because we had a big influx of people in the years which followed World War II we now have many people of different cultures and customs; some Asian, some Afro Caribbean and some African.

To ensure that there was no nastiness going on in the country, the government introduced race relation laws. Alongside these wise precautions there were movements to safeguard people who were not able to compete in our competitive society because they had physical or mental differences of some kind.

So the kind government instructed local Councils to make pavements lower in the places where wheelchairs would be crossing, and instructed that certain toilets were reserved for people who needed to use them, and also gave little blue cards for such people who could drive cars to keep at bay the army of men and women with yellow striped uniforms who prowl along the side walks of streets with yellow lines. We should applaud the different Governments who have presided over these attempts to make us all more tolerant and charitable.

But not all the institutions in our country live up to these noble ideals. Among these institutions I am sad to say is the Holy Catholic Church. Yes, the One True, Holy, Catholic and Apostolic Church which descends from the Apostles.

◇ ◇ ◇ ◇ ◇ ◇

5

When Love At The Heart Of The Gospel Reflects The Same Love At The Heart Of Our Priesthood

ক্তিক্তিক্তিক্তি

I live in a quiet backwater, in an upstairs flat of a building, which bends at an angle of ninety degrees to contain eight similar apartments. Tall trees surround the complex and a carpet of grass, well manicured, spreads between the building and unrolls itself between the further complex of similar apartments towards a tall hedge on the borders of a canal.

As I have mentioned, it is, literally, a backwater. On the canal there are my old friends the ducks. I like to think they followed me from Upholland, but I don't think that is true.

Along the bank of the canal, spaced out at regular intervals, are fishermen. I pass regularly up and down the canal. I have never seen any fish wriggling or panting in any of the baskets ready for them. There are no fisher girls, only fishermen, some of them quite young. I have this picture of Purgatory in my mind as a place where they wait patiently in perfect peace like fishermen along the canal bank or footballers on the substitutes' bench, waiting and waiting.

In the apartments not occupied by priests, there are numbers of men and women. We are not a young group. I do not think that any resident is under sixty years old, and, strangely, there are more unmarried than married.

So there is no karaoke music blasting its way to the night sky, no football under neon lights, no police cars screaming past, no take away plastic left over chucked on the grass, or used beer cans on the doorstep. Fortunately I had the three years' novitiate at Upholland before I came or I would not believe that I was living in present-day England, that somehow I had slipped back one hundred years or so in time... Shaded by tall trees, protected from alien sounds by double-glazing, I live a life of quiet and secluded peace, more or less.

I owe this to the care and forethought of younger priests. Some time in the seventies or eighties a group of young priests raised the funds to provide adequate retirement places for old priests who would otherwise have clung fearfully to the parish house they lived in, because there was nowhere to go. They spoke forcibly that it was justice to give old priests a decent retirement shelter. There is a bond of love and affection binding priests together. Most of us now live on our own, but it is rare to feel lonely.

This is partly because of the support of the people, but it is also because of this bond in the priesthood. We feel welcome in each other's homes. We enjoy each other's company. We welcome priest strangers, African, Asian, Chinese, European, and American... no matter who they are we give them shelter and welcome. We care for each other's welfare. If one goes seriously wrong, we all feel the loss or the shame.

The love at the heart of the Gospel is the love at the heart of the priesthood. We may walk different paths, but we sing to God from the same hymn sheet. It is so different in the England of 2003.

A few weeks ago a woman from one of my previous parishes came to see me. She is a widow. Her children have now grown up and left home. She had a comfortable residence in that parish. She has been driven out of it by wild groups of young men and women who roam the street outside her house; night after night she lived in fear. She shuddered as she talked about the foul language, the taunts, the garbage tipped in her garden, the atmosphere of hate and intimidation.

I know what she describes because I have lived in the same kind of streets and seen the same phenomenon, lived through it, and wondered. There is an evil spirit possessing the twilight world of the drug addicts and alcoholics. It changes the love and idealism of youth into something alien, which drives out love and compassion. Despite all that, it may well be that out of those groups of alienated young people the power of the Holy Spirit may produce the saints who will lead the priesthood itself to a new level of perfection, as the wild flowers grow out of spoil heaps.

6

I Would Happily Award A Knighthood To David Blunkett's Marvellous Guide Dog

৵৴৵৴৵৴৵৴৵৴

I thank God that in this age of swift progress in so many avenues of living, so much thought has been given to the sick and the people who used to be called 'handicapped.' *(I am not sure what the correct term is now).*

Olympic status for people who race in wheelchairs, special schools for children, free medicine, a health service which is probably the best in the world - I could go on.

Many of these benefits have come from the work of pressure groups. Some of them have been introduced because lawyers obtained compensation from Town Councils or firms who tried to practise discrimination. The lawyers have worked hard on these matters, and now the spectre of compensation weighs heavily on the people who think they control things. But do they?

Lurking on the sidelines, on the substitutes' bench, are categories they have overlooked. I was in one parish where the housekeeper always put the teapot on the top shelf of the cupboard. At that time I was addicted to tea. Each morning I had to find a chair to reach the teapot. I told her, but she was a lady who grew so tall that it weakened her concentration.

Again, when I was ordained, the vestment makers Hayes and Finch, Vanpoulles, Ormsby & Co followed customs that had been handed down for hundreds of years. The outer vestment worn at Mass is called a chasuble. As you know, they come in green, purple, white, red and black, according to the kind of Mass and the season of the year. The style, which was traditional, was called 'the fiddleback' by us. I could wear them - they fitted. Now the vestments are not meant to fit normal people.

There's also the growing practice of putting bolts on doors at the top of the door instead of the obvious place. The bigger the door, the higher the bolt. Then someone in the place leaves a note on the vestment press "Please put the bolt on the door before you leave." I thought once or twice "they will put the lock at the top of the door soon." And they have done.

So tabernacles seem to grow taller in modern churches, and Paschal Candles stand in seven-foot candleholders. The head altar boy, who is now in the sixth form, whispers to me at the Easter Vigil: "Father please place the candle in the stand." And I whisper back: "Do it yourself." He says "I'm not allowed to" and I whisper "You are now', and forget that the radio mike is on.

When I was young and foolish, I felt disadvantaged, but I left that behind long ago. I see a robin perched on the branches of the tall trees, which stand dark and bare outside my window in this freezing winter weather. The robin is so much more attractive than the big crows that perch on the top branches.

The crocuses will be out in a few weeks. They are so tiny and yet they are a real joy. The beauty of the world is that there are so many different varieties in nature and in the whole of creation. God is beauty. The creation is beautiful because it reflects him. And so it is with men and women, teenagers and children. God makes them beautiful, their size, shape, hair and face are all different.

It is we who destroy ourselves. We are authors of ugliness. We can destroy landscapes, we can produce ugly music and ugly art.

We can destroy our bodies. We can chase 'freedom' and find ourselves enslaved. I know all this. It is not a theory; I have seen it working out before my own eyes, year after year.

So I don't care about bolts high up on doors or vestments that don't fit or cracked housekeepers. They are just things to laugh at. I don't want compo from any brilliant lawyer. But I do admire people who have faced up to the disadvantages of life and changed the world for the better, even in little ways.

Thank God they are so many in number, and most of them are unknown. But to high profile ones, I would pick out the Home Secretary. We have had blind Home Secretaries before, but it was a different kind of blindness. He must be unique. If I had the job of handing out knighthoods, I would give one to his guide dog. He knows more about politics than any dog in history. But the journalists don't know his language.

7

Tilly Was Caught Up In The Beads Of Her Joyful Mysteries.

In the parish there were three ten-storey buildings, high rise blocks of concrete, built in the second half of the 1950s, and Tilly lived on the ninth floor.

I don't know why they called her Tilly, but everyone did, and when I said her requiem it was Tilly that was written on her coffin. In the hot summer days I would see her from the street, sitting out on the balcony up in the sky, for my eyes were good in those days. I knew the flat because I brought her Holy Communion. I took the lift up to the ninth floor, rang the bell, and went out through the living room to where she was sitting on the deck chair. I picked up a stool and sat beside her.

She was surrounded by flowers in pots. I did not know all their names, but I knew the roses and the dahlias. They filled the still air with scent; in the background was her own rosy and wrinkled face, with the bright eyes and the hair white on top. She was saying the rosary. She was always saying the rosary. She had one of those rosaries they call Irish Horn, and the beads were worn smooth by the passing of the years. I looked out from the balcony, to the dim shape of the Crown on the Cathedral at the top of Brownlow Hill where the old workhouse stood, to the big tower of the Anglican cathedral, out towards the misty shapes of the Welsh hills with the sun shining on the river, which was once the life-blood of Merseyside.

I looked down at the street far below with the long lines of council houses linked together in one long curving crescent. "What do you think about when you say the rosary?" I asked. There was a silence for a while.

"I'm saying the joyful mysteries at present," she said. "I was thinking about the day the policeman knocked on the door in Hopwood Street. He was a big powerful man but we all knew him. He was kind and gentle, sat me down and told me that John had been killed at the docks. I had seven young children. Angels don't always bring good news, but God took care of us. We never had money, but we were happy. I still miss him."

She sighed. "And the second mystery?" I queried. "I was thinking of my granddaughter, Rosie. She came to see me at Easter, she has just qualified to be a doctor. As Our Lady said, 'The Almighty has done marvels for me, Holy is His Name.' I never thought I would see that day."

She was like a bee sucking honey from the mysteries, like the one just now settling on the rose. Her eyes were full of joy. "The third one?" I said. Again the silence. Then: "I was thinking about my son, Terence. He joined the army and married a girl from Garston. He was sent to Germany, and they had army quarters there. She became pregnant, and she went for a scan. They told her the child would be brain-damaged. She was deeply troubled and wanted an abortion, but I offered every decade of the rosary for them. She changed her mind and the child was born. It was perfect."

She knew I was going to ask about the fourth decade, and she anticipated me. "I heard," she said, "that Simeon told Our Lady that she would have a sword of sorrow in her soul. I cannot get Phillip out of my mind. He was my youngest son and I loved him dearly. He was a wild lad but he loved me and I knew it. He was killed on a motorbike on the East Lancs Road. He was just seventeen. He's always on my mind; I re-live the agony as I say the Hail Mary's." Then she told me about the last decade, about the day her Alice was evacuated to Wales in 1940. She was just seven-years-old, but she had made her first communion.

"It was just after her father's death," she said. "It broke my heart. She came back for good in 1945. I met her at Lime Street station and hugged her till her breath nearly left her. She's the one who looks after me now. I say the Hail Holy Queen for all of them living and dead, and for the grandchildren." Again came the long silence and I left her.

The children put the worn-out rosary around her neck when she died a year later. The Requiem Mass was crowded for she was loved by young and old. She was buried in a corner of the cemetery; the bees were busy where the wild flowers were growing.

8

Most Asylum Seekers Don't Have A Sue Ryder Safety Shield.

ఈ≻ఈ≻ఈ≻ఈ≻ఈ≻

In the days when Fr. Cogley was the chaplain to the sick on the Archdiocesan pilgrimage to Lourdes, he asked me to provide him with some help because the number of sick people was large. I felt privileged to be of use, and thereafter, for some years, we worked together. It was at this time I met one of the women patients who left a deep impression on my memory.

She was not tall, her hair was grey, she was under-weight, gaunt, and approximately forty years old. Her back was furrowed by scourges. She was a survivor from a Nazi concentration camp, a Polish woman who spoke broken English, and was in the care of the Sue Ryder Foundation.

Her eyes were dark. They spoke silently about unspeakable things. Years later I went to Auschwitz; the memory still haunts me. I mention this because of a discussion in a group last week where the subject of evil in the world and the non-intervention by God became a central theme. I guess it always does. Even atheists see it is a proof that God does not exist. But, of course, he does.

The answer to the enigma lies somewhere in a deeper understanding of Freedom, of which Jesus said: "If you let my word make its home in you, you will know the Truth, and the Truth will liberate you." So contemplation of the teachings of Jesus, in the Gospel, can set you free. In one of those terrible camps the Gestapo entered a barracks in the evening. There was a boy of fourteen in the shed. They made a noose from a rope and hanged him from the beams. The child took a long time to die because he was thin and underweight from starvation. The prisoners, helpless and in horror, watched the child die. One of them murmured. "Where is God now?" Another one spoke. He said, "He's hanging there, in front of you." His Presence is always there; a multitude of survivors of torture and persecution can testify to that.

I spent the night journey on the train from Lourdes talking with the woman and realised, as she did, the great work that Sue Ryder had done. For that extraordinary woman was alive with the Holy Spirit. Yet, sadly, most asylum seekers who flee to Britain do not have a safety shield like Sue Ryder surrounding them. They can meet the hard face of officialdom. And the British official can be repugnant.

I once lost a passport during a short stop in a Hungarian border town. I visited a market, and when I left it my wallet had gone. I rejoined the coach and managed to pass into Austria without it.

We were due to stay two nights in Vienna. The next morning I borrowed a map of the city and set out to find the British Embassy. Our hotel was on the far side of the river from the city centre. I got a bus to St. Stephen's Cathedral and walked down to the Winter Palace because it was in that quarter that the Embassy was situated.

I found it before midday, down a side street. It was a grim building. A steel door slid open when I gave my postcode and name over an intercom. The office for an interview was small and sparsely furnished; a few chairs, a couch in green leather. Three young men were sitting silently on the chairs. They were poorly dressed, hunched in the chairs, silent and seemingly drained of their spirit. At one end was a counter with a glass screen. I pushed a bell button on the counter. After five minutes a young woman appeared at the far side of the glass. She was tall and slim, dark hair, manicured fingernails. She looked at me with obvious distaste. She said "Yes?" with the way they say it when they mean "No."

I told her my story. I did not expect her sympathy, she did not seem to have any. She wanted proof. I produced a letter from the Viennese police. I had paid 20DM for it. I waited all that day for the passport papers. It was at the end of the evening when she gave them to me. I walked back in the dusk on a bridge some thousand feet above the Danube River. No, I would not like to be a refugee looking for help from Britain. A country that was poorer would perhaps understand me.

9

How The BBC Pulled Out Their Heavies And Funded My Trip To Medjugorje
≪ゐ≪ゐ≪ゐ≪ゐ≪ゐ

Ayrshire is not the most beautiful part of Scotland. In the era when coal mining was its major industry, it must have been a difficult place to live in.

Yet the small villages, which multiplied during the reign of king coal, were close communities. Those who emerged from them were men and women who were tough and resilient. Men like Bill Shankly. But on the whole they were not famous for drama, art or music, not, that is, until the young music composer James Macmillan rose to stardom. His grandfather was a miner, his father a joiner. He joined the choir in the local Catholic Church when he had just made his first Communion. By the age of forty-three he had composed some of the finest music to emerge from the Scottish genius in years.

When Archbishop Rowan Williams is enthroned in Canterbury it will be his choral setting of a poem by George Herbert that will be played. James MacMillan is a dedicated, devout Catholic, it comes out in his work. He was interviewed on ITV by Melvyn Bragg. Melvyn's a good interviewer, and he has a Catholic background. He ended up saying, "Is your Faith a comfort to you or a difficulty? You don't have to answer if you don't want to." It would be a nice question to ask Catholics in different stages of their life ... at Confirmation, in the first years of marriage, in their last sickness. I wonder will God ask us?

It is not easy going public on TV. Sometimes priests are persuaded to take part in programmes or to be interviewed because of something that has taken place in their parish. Usually we get in touch with Peter Heneghan who takes care of media interests for the Archdiocese, and ask him to do it because there are important techniques in appearing on the screen; it is easy to make a mess of it. A great deal depends on the producer. If they are not cynics, and have no hidden agendas it is a big help. I was asked to help with a production for Everyman, which came out on Sunday evenings.

It was a successful programme and attracted a large audience. It was intended to produce it in the interim period between the going of one Archbishop of Canterbury and the appointment of another. Archbishop Runcie was retiring. What would his successor be like, what should he do? They wanted four profiles. They asked four people to write a script. One of those approached was a well-known female novelist who had written very successful novels based on the Church of England. One was a female journalist, married to a vicar. One was an Afro Caribbean gentleman, a university lecturer. Scraping the barrel, and desperate, because time was short, they asked me. The producer was Angela Tilbey. I had met her on a previous programme called 'This is the Day.'

I liked her. She came to the house and pleaded with me. I said "No." I gave her a list of intelligent and literate Catholics with lots of experience. One was in Holland at the time. She went and saw them all and they all said "No." She came back "Don't let me down, you can do it." Like the softie I am, I gave in.

I sat down early one morning and in ten minutes I had written what an Archbishop should do. I sent it off to the

BBC and they said OK. And sent in the heavies. They came, big cameramen, little men with tiny cameras and tape recorders. They followed me to the town centre, to the church, to the industrial estate, into the houses where I saw sick people. Angela was always in the background.

Her last big religious film had been Medjugorje, I had never been there, so I asked her about it. She told me her reactions. They were favourable. She thought the Franciscans were holy men, the visionaries were sincere and transparent. "Do you think Our Lady is appearing there?" I asked. She said. "It's not for me to say. Go and see for yourself." The film went on air a few days before the name of George Carey was pulled out of the hat. I don't think Archbishop Worlock liked it. Monsignor Buckley did. The BBC sent me £500, and I booked a plane to Medjugorje.

10

Suppose This Lent We Opted To Let The Spirit Take Over Our Lives

ഏഏഏഏഏഏ

Lent is like a cold shower. The days before I feel naked and shivering putting a toe into it to see how cold it is.

I understand the cities and villages of the European mainland where they used to celebrate 'carnival' the weekend before Ash Wednesday, dressing up wildly and drinking litres of alcohol so that they can stagger into Lent feeling that they needed a rest from riotous living. But why do I feel like this? The modern Lent in the Catholic Church is a doddle compared to the past.

And if you think the Muslims are hard done by Ramadan, because they cannot eat or drink from sunrise to sunset, just cast your eyes on our past.

For the first nine hundred years the Lenten fast forbade flesh meat, eggs, milk, cheese, butter, and wine. One restricted meal was allowed once a day, only after sunset. So it was a rigorous twenty-four hour ordeal. Add to this, that in Holy week the menu was bread, salt, herbs and water ... after sunset.

A slight modification in the tenth century allowed the one meal to be taken at three o' clock in the afternoon. This was later changed to noon. After the Black Death people were allowed a collation in the evening. Not a lot to cheer about, unless you have been trying to lose weight.

You could excuse them going bonkers at Shrovetide, at the end of Lent when the Easter sun warmed the tiles. The custom of allowing a crust of bread and coffee was allowed in the early years of the nineteenth century. That was how it was when I was young.

I remember the Prefect in my college days coming around the refectory in Shrovetide. He used to look at me, underfed, underweight, undersized and under a lot more, he would rasp 'you are excused from fasting."

You won't believe this, but I resented the dispensation. If you are one of a crowd, you are one of a crowd. And you like to stay like that. It is a phenomenon which goes a long way to explaining why a Muslim in Bahrain would be loathe to be seen drinking or eating in daytime during Ramadan, why people want to join the armed forces in wartime, and young men who had escaped death at the game in Hillsborough when so many young football fans were crushed to death, felt that they also should have died.

That is the kind of solidarity that makes possible the keeping of difficult regimes like the ancient Lenten fast, and makes possible the Muslim practices like Ramadan. It does not begin spontaneously. It begins usually because a law is passed with sanctions attached to it. In other words, fast or take the consequences. The consequences are spelt out.

In the Catholic Church it was mortal sin. In dark little confessionals people mumbled to an unseen authority: "I ate meat last Wednesday. I missed Mass three weeks ago." That was major stuff. You sensed black angels waiting in the shadows to carry you off. But that was law.

Law produced solidarity and, in time, solidarity produced a culture. We became proud of that culture. Suddenly, at the Second Vatican Council it all changed. It was the wind of the Spirit. It wasn't exactly that Catholics were dancing in the streets. The hard liners said: "The Church is going soft."

But last Sunday you heard a prophecy: "No need to recall the past. See I am doing a new deed" (Isaiah 43). Now across the world many Catholics have taken up fasting from food because they want to.

Many thousands have followed the Medjugorje custom of twice-weekly fasting on bread and water. Youth 2000 makes similar demands. Devotees of CAFOD fast every Friday and send the money to the poor. Millions across the world have taken up other forms of fasting - from television, alcohol, tobacco, newspapers, shopping and other addictions. As St Paul says in the letter to the Galatians we are no longer slaves of the law.

We must let the Spirit direct our lives. Live in love, pray, contemplate the suffering and risen Jesus. Then the people with no food in their stomachs will dance in the streets for joy, and the curious crowd will say, "What's got into them?"

11

Gathered For The Last Anointing, Holy Oil Glistened On Her White Forehead.

∽ᅏ∽ᅏ∽ᅏ∽ᅏ∽ᅏ

There was a family meeting about it. The Consultant called them in and made the position clear.

There was no more the hospital could do for Jo. They had used the tried and tested treatment for the sickness, normally there was a 90 per cent success rate, only a 10 per cent failure rate. Unfortunately Jo was in the 10 per cent band. Her system rejected the cure, she was deteriorating rapidly.

Already she was in the intensive care unit and living on a life support machine. Leaving the unconscious young woman, they moved into the waiting room nearby reserved for near relatives of very ill patients.

There they debated the needs of the immediate future. The first question was, should they ask for a priest? The Faith into which they had all been baptised had ceased to be relevant to their busy lives.

This grieved their mother who was very devout. Jo was the youngest member of the family. Her two brothers were struggling to pay their mortgages and the overwhelming priority in their lives was to find the money to support their growing responsibilities.

The seeds of Faith had been planted during the infant school years; some time later the pressures of their mates made it too uncomfortable to be seen practising.

But there was a great deal of love and unity among them all, and for the last two years they had taken their younger sister Jo with them to the big hotel on the Spanish beach. Her mother insisted and they all agreed it would do her "no harm" to send for the priest.

One of their relatives, a friend of mine, was a practising Catholic. They phoned him, he came to see them in the hospital, and there he talked about the power of prayer. They listened respectfully. My friend phoned and asked me if I would anoint the young woman.

I tried phoning the chaplain, but I could not trace him so I picked up the little silver vessel containing the oil of the sick blessed on Holy Thursday and drove to the hospital.

Intensive Care units are unusual. Silence, semi-darkness, figures lying on raised beds with rails around them, leads attached to their bodies, connecting with glass containers above the beds, electronic signals playing continually across the screens, nurses and doctors talking in whispers behind desks with shaded lamps.

Her mother was with her, sitting by her side. She was deeply unconscious. I gave her absolution and then laid my hands on her, poised slightly above her head "Holy Spirit, Healing Power of God come upon her" I whispered. Time seemed to stand still. Her chest rose and fell rhythmically.

I unscrewed the silver vessel, and anointed her. "Through this holy anointing may the Lord in His love and mercy help you with the grace of the Holy Spirit. May the Lord who frees you from sin save you and raise you up."

The holy oil glistened on her white forehead, the wavy lines on the screen beside her moved noiselessly on and on.

"Jesus, ease the sufferings of our sick sister and make her well again in mind and body. Forgive her sins and grant her full health so that she may be restored to your service." I blessed her mother. "Keep praying" I said. I went out through the double doors in to a busy corridor. The words of

St James were beating through my brain "The prayer of Faith will save the sick person", the prayer of Faith, the powerful irresistible spiritual power of the believers.

Maybe that was a bridge too far for this group. I phoned the friend who had asked me to do this. "Phone a network of people, people of faith who understand it in the very centre of their being. It may not be too late."

He listened to me and asked me what had happened. I told him I did not know, but I did know that this was the message I felt I had to give him.

He spent the next hour phoning until he had secured a solid group who could be trusted to pray the "Prayer of Faith." They were believers. They understood the power within their grasp. Week after week he kept them informed of progress, of the day when some kind of return to life took place, a fragile flower, but it was life. He told of the time the doctors moved her out of intensive care.

And he was there when she walked into a healing Mass with the family around her, to thank the Lord who had listened to the prayer.

12

Irish Girls Were Of Course As Flirty And Precocious As Any In The World
⊰⊱⊰⊱⊰⊱⊰⊱⊰⊱

I have not seen the film called The Magdalens, perhaps I never will. It concerns, apparently, the Ireland of fifty or more years ago. To have a baby out of wedlock was treated with intolerance. The mother was the focus of the shame. The father slipped into anonymity. The parents disowned the daughter.

She was forced to take refuge in some new country or new place. If the family did not have the kind of money needed for her safe removal, she was "put away" in the care of 'the nuns.' She went into a soap-dominated future, the soap was not on film, it was on a scrubbing board - the unwed mother worked in the convent laundry. The laundry provided the economic support for the charity.

The baby was handed over to an orphanage until an adoption could be arranged. According to the thinking of the time it seemed to be a good solution. Similar institutions existed in England and met with approval. It was not entirely an Irish problem.

But in Ireland the myth of the pure Irish colleen still existed. Factually it was different. Irish girls were as flirty and precocious as any in the world. There were always unmarried mothers staying with their families, working in offices and shops while nana took care of the child. And none of them were living in fear of being taken away to a nun slave driver in a laundry.

But the idea was meat and drink to a media licking its lips over priests and child abuse, revealing all about bishops who failed to remedy abuse, intent on slaughtering cardinals with Irish names like Murphy or O'Connor.

So the report about vicious Irish convents under the control of Geraldine McEwan (who stars in the film as Rev Mother) was too good to miss. I would not like to be disillusioned about nuns. I have always found them gentle and kind to a frightening degree which I will never reach myself.

When I was a young altar boy there was a convent near the parish church, and the chance of getting a date to "serve at the connie" was actually fought over by the altar servers. This did not denote a growing sense of spirituality. The Sisters offered a cup of hot tea and a plate of cakes at the end of the Mass specifically for the altar server. We scoffed the lot.

Later, at Upholland, I formed the opinion that the Sisters were angels. I read all the books I could about nuns who did heroic things. I came to the conclusion that this height of spirituality that seemed native to religious sisters was way out of my reach.

Yet later I met girls who talked about the nun who gave them the cane, lowered the length of their skirts, cut their hair short or forbade them to go to the Cavern. But I have never met these types. In my innocence therefore I feel sceptical about Sister Geraldine McEwan and her Magdalens. On the other hand, nuns are female and females can be nasty.

There was the case last week when three of us with rucksacks and old boots wandered into a farmyard on the edge of the Lake District. The most intelligent member of this remnant of the Last of the Summer Wine had a map which, he claimed, led us through the farmyard.

I was standing knee deep in sludge when suddenly a woman appeared from nowhere. She was about five feet tall, dressed in an oily pinafore and a big pair of wellies. She was seething and attacked us ferociously for being where we were. I was so scared I felt like diving beneath the sludge and crawling out under the cover of mud. But the other two talked her into a state of calmness.

So I guess women can get like that if they run a laundry for naughty girls and went for them dressed in an oily pinny and wellies; I could see Granada or Channel Four rushing in the cameras. For there is a lot of pride and prejudice about what the press does.

Last Saturday I went with some of my friends and the Prince of Peace Community to a Mass in Westminster Cathedral presided over by the Cardinal. The cathedral was crowded, more than 2,500 people had come. At the end of the Mass Charles Whitehead, the President of the European Renewal Movement, thanked the cardinal. Then the crowd erupted. They thundered applause that became a standing ovation of several minutes. The cardinal was moved deeply. The crowd were not only saluting him, they were giving a message to the critics.

13

That Journey Affected Me Deeply. There Is Something Special About Walsingham.

✥✥✥✥✥✥✥✥✥✥

I found today a diary dated back to 1996 and realised that, on April 7th of that year I left parish life. It was the end of 54 years of life in parishes, through the darkness of the Second World War, the bewildering changes to the Church, its liturgy, and the changing face of society.

Thirty of those years had been spent as parish priest at St Joseph the Worker in Kirkby. I left after the evening Mass on that Easter Sunday, leaving almost everything behind me, and drove along the M62 to Leeds. I was exhausted and grief stricken. I knew it was the best thing for the parish and for myself, but I was apprehensive about what the future would hold. I was following the principle that I had been given, that once I left the parish I would not return except under duress. A new priest must be given space and time to make changes and select new leaders. My presence, even if infrequent, would do damage and would be wrong. But there was something of the experience of dying in it, leaving the people I loved and uncertain of the future.

The one bright spot was that I knew I had a room at Upholland College. I had grown to love it and the people who worked there. In the days that followed I moved on to Middlesbrough to stay with Fr Pat Keogh. Walking on the North Yorkshire moors, I knew that I had two immediate objectives.

One was to walk to Walsingham to thank Our Lady for all she had done for me in my years of preparing for the priesthood and the subsequent decade. I would do it alone. It was to be an act of thanksgiving. The second wish was to spend part of the winter on an island which was remote and subject to the wild winds and high seas. There I could find God and rethink my life. But Walsingham came first.

Knowsley Community College paid for my boots and the Gore-tex outer clothing. Early in July I set out. That journey affected me deeply. When I returned I wrote a reflective diary based on the mini-recorder I had taken with me. I typed it at hot speed while the vivid memories were still fresh. Then I left it. It was my personal memoir, not for publication. Someone plucked it off my desk and asked, "May I read it?" I agreed. It vanished and reappeared months later. It was typed and re-typed. Friends asked for an appraisal of the footpaths. Meanwhile the arrival of the Labour Government opened up new footpaths across the country. It meant a further appraisal. I made excursions to check out the pathways and wrote them up. The pressure mounted to have it printed.

One of my friends, Anthony, from Penketh near Warrington, produced a whole copy of what it should look like on a computer disc. He had recently retired from Ford's and spent a whole year working on the maps.

In London, in the Hall of Westminster Cathedral during an exhibition of Catholic culture, I stopped at a bookstall and talked with the distinguished gentleman who manned it. He said he was Tom Longford, and that he was the Director of Gracewing, a publishing firm specialising in books of Catholic interest.

He asked to see what Anthony had produced and agreed to publish this little book because the Holy Spirit uses events and objects which look unimportant. Life, history, is more than a series of coincidences. Walsingham has been a centre of pilgrimage for nearly a thousand years. It is sacred to the memory of an apparition of the Blessed Virgin in the opening years of the second Christian century.

Its revival shortly before the beginning of the third century is not a coincidence. It has a deeper meaning than that. It is a sign that this nation must find again its Christian roots. It is time for change, time for an end to creeping paganism. As I write, two powerful armies have invaded the ancient lands of the bible. Between the rivers Tigris and Euphrates lie the cities of Baghdad and the remains of Babylon. From the desert land Abraham was moved by the word of God. Here he began his long journey of Faith. It seems, now, that most of the world is aghast at this act of war and many in our country have divided views. Time to change the heart of this nation. There is something special about Walsingham!

14

Many Like Him, Young Men And Women, Give Everything They Have For An Ideal

Some miles away from the city of Maastricht in the south of Holland, in a green belt surrounded by tall trees, there is a war cemetery.

Two flagpoles just inside the impressive stone gate fly the stars and stripes of the United States of America. The driveway entrance is shaded by the trees, so that the effect on emerging from them is similar to coming out of a tunnel into open country; what meets the eye is unnerving. As far as vision can reach, on grass laundered and tended like a football stadium, are thousands of little white crosses. On each cross is the name of a young American killed in the Second World War. There is also a large pavilion at the entrance with graphic details of the battles for the crossing of the Maas and the Rhine.

There is a sense of the sacred about all cemeteries, but especially about war cemeteries. I had seen these young men on the streets of Ashton-in-Makerfield, in the cafes and pubs of wartime Liverpool.

Some of them had visited my parents' home. They were so self-possessed, cheerful and generous. They had never been outside America before, they did not know what the future held for them. They loved their American home. It was not threatened in any way by war. But if they had not come to Europe life here would be different.

"No greater love has anyone than to lay down his life for his friend." Jesus was speaking about himself when he said that. The thought of what happened in that week which changed the world in the year 33AD dominates the thinking of all Christians world wide, and has done so for two thousand years. It was the fact that the Word made Flesh took this path to lead the world from darkness into light, from slavery into freedom that remains part of the mystery of Holy Week.

To die for a world. To die "so that sin might be forgiven" was the climax of his mission and the ultimate expression of love. In this holy time, I include with him the men and women who struggle and die now in the desert lands from which Abraham came. These are the Bible lands, Babylon and its rivers, the mighty Tigris and Euphrates, which figure so large in the dealings of God with men in the Bible story.

The Americans who once again are far from their homeland, and the British and Australian men, and the poor Iraqis who fight because it is their own land. They are all caught up in this mystery of Passion. Death and Resurrection.

I still see, vividly, in the garden of memories, the tall figure of Michael Casey smiling from a German Volkswagen car, dressed in his army uniform with his red beret on his head, and then in his changed garb of white cassock in the silences of Wonakom in the heartlands of Nigeria. Then standing in the doorway of a supermarket in Bootle so that he could say "good morning" to the people who crowded in there but did not crowd into his church. When he joined the army they knew they had a treasure. 'Sign here, Father, they said right away". When I made tentative approaches they looked at me and suggested they were not that hard up.

Michael joined armies because he loved the world, and knew it was one way to make the world a better place. It was the same ideal which sent him to Africa for fifteen years.

There are many like him, young men and women, who follow an ideal and give their all for it. Some of them will be in the desert of Iraq, some of them will be in Parliaments and other Government buildings around the world forfeiting their reputation and their influence for the sake of their conscience.

For such, also, was the world of men and women who swirled around the hill of Calvary when the Saviour of the world was being lifted up. It is not only in the Mass that the Passion of Christ is being re-enacted.

15

It Was For Times Like This That God Gave Us Guardian Angels.

On a grey Saturday afternoon five days ago, I came out of a grim, old building erected by Edward III, King of England in the fourteenth century. I was just nosing around, putting in the time between some lectures. I looked across to the Houses of Parliament, and began the short journey back to Westminster Cathedral. I cut through the gardens of Westminster Abbey. Despite the time of the year, and the rain in the cold of the early evening, the number of people on the streets was impressive.

Among the throng was a short, stumpy woman, aged about sixty. With her was a little girl who could have been three years old. Obviously it was the grannie and the grandchild, and they caught my eye because the little one was dressed in bright clothes and she was skipping and dancing with delight because she was alive and with nanna. She stood out in the gathering gloom against the ancient grey stone of the Abbey and the dark winter clothing of the pedestrians like a luminous petal floating on the breeze.

Suddenly she darted away from her guardian and began running around the couples and the threesomes. At times they parted and let her through. She picked up speed, left the Abbey Gardens and hurtled towards the open road. The grandmother chased after her, but her legs were short and her body was heavy. Now the child had left the safety of the gardens and she was darting along the pavement of the road, perilously near the endless traffic of London at teatime. I felt the panic of the old lady, and began chasing her myself. Away in the distance I saw her, running towards a knot of other women and children. I called to them to stop her, but they parted and let her through. I gave it up. After all, it was for times like this that God gave us Guardian Angels. But, in addition, I realised that in the modern climate, no-one was likely to stop a child unless they had a certificate to do so and an approving audience to watch them. This means that the same rules which safeguard a child might be the very reasons why an innocent little one dies on the street.

I walked back ruminating about this. There are so many occasions when there is this clash of interests, of rights versus obligations. And they make life as difficult for the young people as they do for the adults.

Thus, later that evening in the centre where the conference was being held, there was a panel of experts to answer the questions of the young. 'The young' ranged from eleven or twelve to sixteen or eighteen. They had sent in some of the questions they wanted to ask. The time allotted for the session was approximately 45 minutes. The first two questions took up almost the whole of the allotted time.

The first question was simply "Do un-baptised people, or people outside the Christian Church, go to hell?" The answer to that is "No." Children understand "No." And it satisfies. But as they get older, in our English climate, it does not satisfy.

A Minister of State, answering questions, never says Yes or No. Rather than do that, they change the question. That confuses. It also fills up time without answering the question and life loses its simplicity. So, to cover every facet of a very deep problem, the answer to that first simple question took twenty-five minutes. I would guess that the eleven, twelve's and thirteen's in the group had lost it by then.

The second question was about alternatives to Christianity such as Witchcraft, Wicca, New Age cults. "Is it alright to engage in them?" I thought that required a simple answer. But I was wrong. To the audience and the panel it was not simple. But where does all this confusion get anybody? Is there no such thing as solid truth any more? Is it all a matter of opinions in which one is as good as another, and no one takes responsibility in case some one else gets offended?

For we live in a world in which too few take responsibility because of the fear of what might follow. And then, there are a multitude of little people dancing and laughing their way to the edge of spiritual nothingness; like the child who escaped from the gardens of Westminster Abbey. So thank God for the Apostle's Creed. There's no waffle in that.

Little Ways

Little ways to show you care, are not so hard to find.
They do not have to cost a lot, or stay just in your mind!
A promise kept, so people know you will not let them down.
A kindly deed, a word of praise, a smile and not a frown.
These little ways to show you care will make you cared for too.
For those who like your little ways, will copy what you do.
A cup of tea, a shared meal, a door held while you pass
And kinder still, the dear friend who remembers you at Mass.
In little ways the world becomes a better place to live.
For no-one's poor in "little ways". We have so much to give.

P.Williams

16

She Had Carried Her Cross In Silence For Long Enough.

ക്കക്കക്കക്കക്ക

There was a woman from the south end of the city who came to live in the parish.

She was a widow, her husband had died the previous year and she was still mourning his loss. She had six children, two had already married but the four younger children were still making their way through the schools. One of the brightest had her eyes fixed on the university.

All the children had been baptised and the good mother had been with them at their baptisms, their first communions, and, when they took place, their weddings. She accompanied them to Mass but never received Holy Communion.

When I asked her about this, she was non-committal; after a while I gave it up because I knew that she knew something that was secret to her, and everyone has a right to their secrets. But, leaving all that religious practice problem aside, she was always there at the school gate to welcome the youngest member of the family when she came out, she supported the weekly Bingo session, she helped at the Christmas Fair and all the other mini efforts to raise cash for the hard up parish. She gave pullovers to kids who were 'perished with cold', every weekend she secretly fed an old man down the street who had given up cooking.

Everyone loved her. Some of the superior ones said "It's a pity she's a Protestant" but most told them to move on and grow up. "She's better than a lot of Catholics," they said. It was the era where, in this part of a complex world, they divided people into Protestants or Catholics, and Reds or Blues. The grey areas were still in shadow. They had not yet come out into the light.

The years passed and she became old, beginning to take care of grandchildren, more and more of them. She began to feel pain in her back and lungs. She went to the doctor, he sent her to hospital. They diagnosed cancer and the long struggle began to cling on to life. X-ray, chemotherapy, scans, more scans, and periods of remission when all the family rejoiced and she put on weight. Then a growing feeling of fatigue and loss of weight: the struggle became too much. The cancer was back and it was aggressive.

One evening in the late springtime, two tear-stained girls came to see me. "My Nan is not well, she wants to see you," they said. I picked up the Oil of the sick. "I wonder...?" Then, following my instinct, I went into the church and took the Viaticum out of the tabernacle.

Outside the house, in the small strip of front garden, there was a group of young men. If I had been riding on a donkey they would have strewn branches in front of me. "She's very sick," they said. They had beer cans with them, and some were smoking.

In the house were similar crowds of women. They showed me to the sick room. She was dying. There was a blessed candle on the table beside her. "I want you to hear my confession and anoint me," she said. The girls moved out and closed the door. "Are you a Catholic?" I asked. Her face had shrunk, her lips were dry and caked. I held a small glass of water to her lips and she tried to smile.

"I was baptised in the workhouse on Brownlow Hill," she whispered. "When I grew up, I once asked a priest if I could make my First Communion, but he wanted my baptism certificate. I was too ashamed to tell him that I was baptised in the workhouse. I never went back. I never asked again. My poor mother was Irish and she was destitute. She died in the workhouse. But I know she loved me. I did not want to shame her."

I gave her absolution, and anointed her there and then. In that bedroom she made her First Communion. I remember looking down at her lying wrapped in peace. She had carried that cross in silence for many long years. Now she had told her secret and awaited the Resurrection. Some hours later she was dead.

The old workhouse on Brownlow Hill became the Curial Offices. Now it is abandoned and empty, clothed in the red brick of an old Victorian building. It is an empty shell, like the empty tomb. On the pavements outside, the future generation of University academics pass by.

God grant that their idealism will one day eliminate, across the world, the harsh destitution that once lay hidden behind the redbrick walls.

17

"What Do You Have That I Haven't?" Now Is The Time To Speak Out
~~~~~~~~~~~~~~~~~~~~

It's a truly Christian impulse to leap for joy and sing out loud when Lent ends and the sorrows of Holy week give way to Resurrection.

It's daffodil time 'beside the lake, beneath the trees.' It's the time for Alleluia, for as Fr Tom Leigh wrote: "We are the Easter people and Alleluia is our song."

People who had been fasting breathe in once again the mouth-watering air of freshly baked cakes floating out of bakeries. Men disappear into dark pubs from which they had been banished on Ash Wednesday. The roads are full of travellers going to see someone else. Airports and train stations are busy; the Christian people are celebrating.

Praise be to God. Praise be to Jesus Christ, The Risen One, the Victorious, the Light of the world. Jesus is Lord.

Banish out of the country the miserable meanies who refuse to sell hot Cross buns in case someone doesn't like them. The ugly people who tried to rule out Christmas because they think some Arab millionaire might not go into their shops. They are like the humourless Calvinists of the so-called Reformation who whitewashed the walls of churches, destroyed frescoes of real beauty and smashed statues all through the length and breadth of this land. They did it in the name of "religion."

But the faceless destroyers of today do it in the name of business. Somewhere in the background also are the atheists, secularists, and Satanists who set out to destroy the Christianity on which our country's culture is based, and, indeed that of the whole of Western and Eastern Europe.

That is why we must declaim ever louder and louder that Jesus is Risen! He is Alive. We must declare it in the houses of the people, in the streets and squares of our cities, in our media and in the witness of our lives. Jesus is Risen, He is the Light of the World. He is the Way, the Truth and the Life. The celebration of Easter, that is, the passing from death to life, signifies believing in the resurrection.

The Church began because the Resurrection was proclaimed with the power of the Holy Spirit. It was proclaimed by the Witnesses. Scientific research came after belief, not before it.

There are people who do not believe it because they have never heard about it. There are people who have heard it, but shrug it off because it could hurt their life style. There are people who hear it, but the people who tell them do not have the conviction given by the Holy Spirit. But I believe, and You believe, We believe. We are the Easter people. Alleluia Jesus is Risen. He is the Lord. People understand simple statements.

I saw a man standing, waiting for a train. He had a black leather jacket, he was young and tall, he had a kind of earring only it was through his lower lip. He had fair hair and deep blue eyes. Written in large white letters on the back of his leather jacket was his message. It read "F... you" It was simple and horrible. I went to him and said. "Why have you got that thing written on your back?" He said, "Because it is what people say to me." I pleaded with him "Please, don't be like that. It is so insulting. It hurts us." He was not angry. He looked at me, and he knew I meant it. His train had come in. He went to it, and the doors closed behind him. The train moved off.

I was in the parish centre in St Mary's, Woolton, when Paul McCartney announced a new song. John Lennon read out the words, and I watched fascinated as two hundred plus teenagers twirled and twisted to the beat singing "Money can't buy me love."

That was a proclamation. It was simple, unsophisticated. But along with proclamation must go joy.

There is innocence about joy. I don't mean the kind of joy that children show when they do cartwheels and slide down glassy slopes squealing with excitement. It is more subtle than that. It shines out of people. It has very deep roots in a spirit filled with innocence and peace, in an affluent and cultured country like modern England, where too many people look and feel like cold, soggy tea bags, the people of joy stand out.

Many look at them, mystified "What have you got that I haven't?" It is time to speak out.

18

Too Many Divisions, Uncertainties And With No Central Authority?

At the western end of Glen Orchy, in the Highlands of Scotland, within sight of majestic Ben Cruachan, and on the north east end of Loch Awe, lies the small village of Dalmally.

It is one of the remote rail stations on the line which goes from Glasgow to Oban, winding its way through remote valleys in the legendary landscape that enriches the Scottish Highlands. In such a romantic setting is the hunting lodge named Craig Lodge.

Craig Lodge, for years, belonged to the family of Calum McFarlane Barrows. It was in his company, trailing behind him perilously on a mountain path which led upwards via fourteen stations of the Cross made of stones from the mountain and small plaques of copper bearing the name and outline of each Station, that he told me the extraordinary events which led to Craig Lodge passing out of his possession to the possession of Our Lady Queen of Peace.

How that radiant Lady moved into the property market is a tale worth telling. I know he won't mind me telling it. I was too insecure at the time to ask his permission. I was wearing two odd shoes which were very old and, without fell boots or trainers, I wobbled on the narrow, rocky path.

He told me that his parents, initially, were Scot Presbyterian. His father was a classical scholar of no mean quality. He had been an outstanding pupil of Eton Public School, and began his career as lecturer and teacher of classics. He felt called by God to leave the profession and went to University to study theology. He was ordained to the Presbyterian ministry and began his work in an extensive Highland parish. By this time he was married and six children were born. He became ever more unsure that the Presbyterian faith was fully authentic Christianity. Too many divisions, too many uncertainties. No final central authority.

His father's search led him to the almost unthinkable conclusion that only the Catholic Church was authentic. He resigned his post and entered the Catholic Church.

Six months later his wife, Calum's mother, did the same. The children also were baptised into the Catholic Church. His parents lost their friends, they were rejected, and faced virtual poverty.

It was from this heroic background that Calum inherited Craig Lodge. In 1988 Calum went with his wife to Medjugorje.

There, they were inspired to leave Craig Lodge and hand it over to Our Lady to become a House of Prayer. They did just that. He told me these things coming down from the fourteenth Station and I saw him ahead of me, striding on the strong firm legs of a mountain man, with his face bronzed from the wind and the rain; there was something of eternal youth about him.

Now Craig Lodge is run by a community. The leader of the community at present is a young woman possibly in her early thirties. She took religious vows in the presence of the community and the bishop of the diocese. She is the first to do this. The community consists of young people who pledge two years of their lives to the apostolate of the house of prayer and the people who come to it.

I spoke to one of them, a young student whose name, I think, was Julie. She told me how she had taken these two years to be more certain of what she wanted from life itself. She is one of a stream of young men and women who have served Craig Lodge.

Not all who apply are suitable for the strenuous existence involved, because there is a monastic quality about the rule to be kept. All those applying are given a short trial term so that they can make their minds up, and so that the community itself can assess their suitability.

Deep in the soul of the Scottish people, as in the innermost soul of the people of Britain, the Spirit of God is moving, creating something new and irresistible. The work of the Spirit is silent and hidden because it resounds in the depths, not on the surface.

Craig Lodge is not an isolated phenomenon. One of the visionaries from Medjugorje came here. In the garden of the house, they say, the Blessed Virgin appeared to her.

After a Mass of spiritual healing on our final night, our group went in a torchlight procession to that garden saying the rosary. And there in that privileged garden, under the full moon, as American tanks entered Baghdad, we sang the Salve Regina.

19

When We Seek Out Spiritual Comfort We Are Often Recalling Past Events.

❧❧❧❧❧❧❧❧❧❧

I don't know if anyone else gets periods of prayer change. I mean the time when a favourite prayer gets dislodged by another one which is pushing for priority.

To make progress means accepting change. So for some time now, I have become more and more intrigued with the Apostles' Creed. I know that for many of us Catholics it is well down the charts, but I think we have lost something.

There is an elemental granite feel about it. Carved out, impervious to the winds of change and the vagaries of time. Rock bottom proclamation: "I believe in God, the Father, Almighty, Creator of heaven and earth."

The scientists and astrophysicists have done a great service to thought by their researches into the beginnings of our world. But they cannot explain who or what began it all.

When they leave out a Supreme Intelligence behind the act of creation, they ask the innocent public to make an act of faith in themselves. But, no, thank you, Mr. Hawkins and all your faithful followers. I do not need you because "I believe in God. Creator of Heaven and Earth." Every statement of this unusual prayer unlocks different agendas. The one attracting me at the moment is the phrase "He will come to judge the living and the dead." And what has focused it in my mind is a constant experience of past sins coming back to haunt our world as if their ghosts are still floating around the cosmos and need to be put to rest, and that, finally, only Jesus the Lord can do it.

You get this recent one about an Irish solicitor who was shot years ago. It was never properly investigated. Now it seems that the British army worked with the Ulster paramilitaries and the police force (RUC) to assassinate him. The sins of the past.

Or the case of Joseph Mugabe in Zimbabwe going manic and crucifying the nation. The first symbols of his going overboard were the expulsion of the white farmers. The people of Africa were silent about it. The non-African people were seething. But everyone knew, beneath the surface, that the white farmers should not have been there in the first place.

History is full of it. Who killed Julius Caesar? Was Richard III innocent? Was Guy Fawkes framed by James the first's MI5? Who shot JFK? So it goes on and on. 'The ghosts of the past.' Justice must be done.

But this works on a personal level also. So often men and women who come for some kind of spiritual help will talk about what happened in their past life. It arises so often in the ministry of healing. It is for this very special reason that I like to have priests available at all healing Masses. At one in the Cathedral it is especially necessary because of the large numbers who attend. It is not that people are not forgiven. It is the ghost of the past rather than the feeling of being unforgiven. It takes a direct intervention by the Holy Spirit to bring the inner peace that is needed.

General Absolution has its place in Christian life, and the huge public support for it demonstrates that. In our country the problem is deep seated because many people are outside the immediate influence of any Christian church, and it affects the whole of their lives.

I was crossing the car park of a shopping precinct recently. A young lady was backing out her car. I waited because I know it is not easy backing out cars.

She stopped the manoeuvre and opened the window. Her face was angry "Make up your mind," she shouted. So I walked behind the car and began to cross the car park again. This seemed to infuriate her. She opened the other window and made a rude remark. I thought it over as I was walking. There was something inside her; something which had nothing to do with driving, and suddenly my waiting had triggered it off. There was a deep-down loss of spiritual peace. She was only a symbol, a modern Ezekiel.

But only the Holy Spirit can open up the windows of the world that peace might enter when justice is done.

20

The Atmosphere Of Decay Showed All The Signs Of Hopelessness.

∽ઌ৵ઌ৵ઌ৵ઌ৵ઌ৵ઌ৵

I was sitting in my little yellow car in one of the areas of Skelmersdale, watching a man in a yellow council overall picking up rubbish with a grab at one end which opened and closed over plastic bags and tattered receipts. Putting aside the fear that he might be coming nearer and that the scratched little car might be the next victim of the grab, I became aware of the poverty of the place.

In the second half of the last century there was a flurry of new ideas on town planning. The planners combined with architects. The architects were coming off a production belt from new universities. The new universities were full of young men and women who dreamed dreams of greatness. The town councillors huffed and puffed, objected and recommended. The results locally were Speke, Kirkby, Netherley, Cantril Farm, and Skelmersdale. They were all different. There is one common factor. People with hope and joy, people with abiding peace in their hearts will affect an area in a way that is strikingly different, to the effect when others move in to a similar area and do not have those qualities.

One area blossoms, the other rots. This area where I sat in the car, as the dark clouds and rain intensified the atmosphere of decay, showed all the signs of hopelessness, poverty, despair. The boarded up shops, the derelict dwellings, the littered pavements, the weary women dragging shopping trolleys. They might have moved in with optimism, but the environment sucks it out of them, and the area sinks. I have seen it so often. The miracle is that there are children who come from such areas and still retain belief and trust in the God who loves them. But it is hard and there are not too many who emerge. In Britain the juvenile centres for offenders is full of those who don't.

Go well down the scale to places like Palestine where millions are oppressed and robbed of their own lands, and you produce suicide bombers, and all such areas of hopeless poverty and deep injustice breed nests of so-called terrorists. "O Lord, that the heavens would open, the clouds part and reveal the Redeemer." The song we sing in the season of Advent becomes a song for the whole year. But the Lord does listen. "I will take away the heart of stone and give you a heart of flesh." The valley of dry bones will yet feel the breath of the Spirit and see the bones come together and stand like an army on its feet, as the prophet Ezekiel said.

This is always the promise of Pentecost. How grateful I am that we are able to celebrate, in our cathedral, reconciliation and healing just before this great Feast of Renewal. Everything is possible for God. His power is the same today as it was on the day that St. Peter and the eleven emerged from the solitude and shade of the room they had shared to the bright streets of Jerusalem and overwhelmed by the power of the Holy Spirit began an unrivalled change in the hearts of men and women, accompanied by signs and wonders.

Energised by this thinking, I drove to the banks of the canal at Appley Bridge, put on a pair of boots and walked. The stretch of canal between Appley Bridge and Parbold must be one of the most beautiful in the whole 200 miles of the Leeds and Liverpool canal. By this time the sun was shining and the May blossom hung in clusters on the hedges. We shall yet change the hearts of men and women, change the graffiti on the subway walls, children will walk to school as they once did, and play in the streets and courts of our towns, flower baskets will decorate the new areas, and burglar alarms vanish from the houses.

It is now, in this present time, possible to harness the immense forces set free by modern technology, that the whole world be raised from destitution, malnutrition, from illiteracy, despotism and injustice. That Muslim, Christian and Jews, will join hands across the world and sing together a love song to the one who created our beautiful world. Then the young men and women, with hope in their heart will look up and not ask how can this happen, but why not?

21

"We Need Bridges, Not Walls."

ခ်ာခ်ာခ်ာခ်ာခ်ာခ်ာ

My phone rings. A female voice speaking in an accent which I cannot distinguish tries to sell me something I have never heard of, and maybe I am not hearing! I have the feeling that they are phoning from India, or China, the Philippines, Indonesia. I have no idea what they are talking about. However I do feel sympathetic.

If they are in fact phoning from long distances overseas and continents, it is because they are from a poor country and some English-speaking firm has commissioned them to phone around the world. They are so commissioned because they are poor and they accept wages unacceptable to Europe.

I am glad this is happening, not because I agree with people being underpaid, but because it is the beginning for them of a new world, and their conditions will only improve when they are given some hope of economic prosperity. The motives of the capitalist are not noble, but they are the people who explore the far distant areas of the world in search of business, where more cautious people would not take that risk.

I try to be patient and kind with the female voice. Behind the voice is a child of God with a story that needs to be told and understood. What is the Spirit saying to our world with all this incredible spread of information worldwide, other than that we all live on one planet and are related to each other across cultures and languages?

Only in our age, in our new era of vast technological growth, can I begin to understand why Jesus, on the brink of the one act which changed the world, his death and resurrection, left only one unyielding command: "A new commandment I give you, that you love one another as I have loved you. By this will all men know that you are my disciples if you have love one for another."

As Pope John Paul II said, when he heard that the Israeli government had ordered a spread of the big wall around Jerusalem "We need bridges, not walls." And the unexpected answer Archbishop Tutu gave when the BBC asked him how he thought the Coalition leaders should move forward on the handing over of power to the Iraqis: "The first step is that the Coalition should humbly apologise to the people of Iraq for the illegal invasion of their country."

Is there the faintest possibility of such a thing? Imagine Christmas 2005: "This Christmas, in the name of all my people," says Queen Elizabeth, "I humbly ask the pardon of all the people of India for our three hundred years of occupation, the people of Africa for the evils of our colonial systems, the people of Ireland for the centuries of cruel oppression."

It would probably be the swansong of the Royalty. But what a good way to go! Pope John Paul did such a thing solemnly, in the Coliseum of Rome at the time of the millennium. Many of the cardinals disagreed with him. But it was a gesture of great power. And he is still there. Reconciliation involves climbing down; recognition at the very heart of the matter that I myself contributed to the evil that fell on someone else; and searching for the person and telling him that I deeply regret it.

A short time ago one of the 'Travelling' people came to see me. A big man he was, all of six feet, built like a tower block in a city. He had the nose of a heavy drinker. I like him; he is my friend. He told me he was selling television sets, that he buys them in a warehouse second hand, and sells them door-to-door.

I asked him "Are they good?"

"They are," he said.

"All of them?" I then asked.

He paused. "There was one I sold to an old man two days ago," he admitted, "I think it was a dud."

"How much did he give you?" I asked. "One hundred pounds" he said. "You should call back and see him and offer him his money back," I said.

He looked hard at me, and then he said, "I will."

He phoned me the next night. "I saw the old man," he said. "I gave him the money back. I let him keep the telly." I felt his pride in the act, coming over the airwaves.

"You did well," I said. "You will be blessed and so will your family."

I haven't seen him since. The act brought peace to both men. Of course the "Traveller" is a simple man. He is uneducated, illiterate. Our people are very highly educated and sophisticated. But those qualities are not necessarily the best for entering the Kingdom of Heaven.

22

Madeira 1994

❦❧❦❧❦❧❦❧❦❧

On Tuesday May 20th I said my farewell to Mgr. Tom McKenna as his mortal remains were laid to rest in the cemetery at Birchley. For me it was not without some emotion. We had many experiences together, especially in the long holidays that he planned meticulously many months before.

The last of these was in Madeira. I think the year was 1994. On the second day after our arrival he wanted to follow a footpath which began high up in the mountain country which made up the greater part of the island. The footpath spirals down what seems to be a very large extinct volcano to a small village on the floor of the valley some 4000 feet below. I had grown accustomed to using a video camera to record our holidays together. In the winter months we used to look at the footage and relive the summer days on hills, in valleys, on mountain paths, in ancient churches and obscure mountain villages,

On this clear warm day in Madeira we took a bus for part of the journey to the mountain path. It dropped us not too far from the summit; we stopped and ate what we had brought in the rucksacks. Tom walked more slowly than I. I took pictures of him walking down the path, his sturdy figure and the rucksack fitting snugly into his shoulders, the well-worn boots moving rhythmically downwards towards the distant village below us. I waited for him at a point where the path was dangerously narrow. Then I went ahead so that I could film him coming around a corner. It was a point where the path broadened out. There were pine trees and shade. I waited.

Time passed and he did not appear. I assumed he had stopped for some reason and I went back to look for him. The more I climbed back the more uneasy I became. There was no sign of him or of any of his belongings. I knew then that he had fallen and I felt a great sorrow sweep over me a sense of total helplessness.

I looked down into the abyss. It was not sheer perpendicular, but nearly so. There were bushes in places, growing out of the rock. I prayed to Our Lady. I always seem to fall back on her in an ultimate crisis. Then I shouted his name and it echoed in the stillness. I shouted again. This time I heard his voice, he was on a ledge, he could not move. It seemed a long way down. It could be five hundred feet, maybe a thousand. "I'm going for help," I shouted "Don't move". I went down to the village, but it took time. I cannot speak Portuguese. I found a man who could talk French, and he was in charge of a small bar. He was an angel. He phoned through to Funchal, which is the capital of Madeira. He told me the mountain rescue would come. I waited.

The hours dragged as I waited and prayed. I did not know if Tom could survive a night on a ledge some three thousand feet up on a mountainside, for this was November. It was dark when at last they came, a minibus full of young athletic men with ropes and torches. I went up the mountain path with them. I was hungry and exhausted but they helped me to move at speed, up and up through the darkness. At last we came to the pine trees. I said, "It was near here." I went up a short distance and once again I prayed to the Mother of

God. Then I shouted his name; suddenly, very faint and distant, I heard his voice.

The young men disappeared down the mountain waving torches and shouting. They found him and brought him up in a canvas stretcher. I saw his face, he was unconscious, it was under the fir trees and in the light of a full moon. At the foot of the mountain an ambulance was waiting and the police cars, with the blue lights turning in the darkness.

People from the village lined each side of the path, and as we came down they were clapping. The police car took me to the hospital. Doctors and nurses were waiting for him. Just before dawn I saw him as they brought him out of the theatre, he was bandaged and unconscious. The surgeon spoke English. He said to me "He will be alright." Some days later Tom talked about it. He said, "I think I had a black out. I do not remember anything except that twice, on the ledge I came back to consciousness and they were the times when I heard your voice." For nine years after that Tom gave joy to many people, but he had walked his last footpath.

23

The Healing Of Christ Also Evangelises The Believers And The Doubters.

◈◈◈◈◈◈◈◈◈◈◈

As I came out of the Cathedral, after the Mass of Consecration for Bishop Tom Williams, I met a former parishioner and asked for her reactions. She confessed that at one time she had no particular attraction to the Cathedral. She had thought that other Cathedrals were better, but after the experience of the Mass for Chrism celebrated in the Cathedral on the Wednesday before Easter and this Consecration Mass, both being crowded, and crowded with the normal mix of people who are the back-bone of Catholicism in the Liverpool Archdiocese, she found herself marvelling at the beauty and dignity of our Metropolitan Cathedral.

I had walked on Tuesday from Central station via Bold Street and Hardman Street and approached along Hope Street and realised just how effective is the new construction taking place at the front of the Cathedral. As time passes and the extraordinary talent of Sister Anthony and her group of workers have transformed the inside of the building, the side chapels have added to the growing beauty of the interior, and the choir and organ are becoming renowned locally, nationally and internationally, the Cathedral is becoming a fitting symbol of the vitality of Catholicism on Merseyside and in the diocese as a whole.

I know I'm going on a bit, but this is being written on the evening of the consecration Mass and my mind is still meditating on the experience. I guess also that my mind is moving forward to June 6th, the night of our healing Mass in the same Cathedral. We will not, of course, have the choir and the organ, or the solemnity of the Consecration Mass. But going by past experience the same kind of crowd will be there, with one very significant difference; many of those who come will be representing the Christ in His Passion.

There will be many victims of cancer, which is endemic in Lancashire and Merseyside, many sufferers from bone disorders of the back, of the legs, of the hips, the neck. Many will come with heart conditions, with respiratory problems. Many with deep depression and a feeling of guilt or rejection.

Hundreds will come to pray for those of their friends and relatives who are too sick to come. They come to intercede for their loved ones. They ask to carry the blessing given them to be carried back to one they represent. They come, men, women and children, young and middle-aged and old.

A Catholic historian, Eamon Duffy, wrote a book titled 'The Stripping of the Altars' which in one paragraph talks about the throngs of sick and disabled and poor who crowded to the great shrines of England in the ages before the desecration of those shrines in the 16th century. Of course, that was before the great modern reforms in medical practice, the advancement of science and the gift of the NHS. So why do they still come? Only they know.

The deep faith of the people sees beyond the gifts of science and technology to the whole world of the Spirit, which is a world beyond that of materialistic science, beneficial though it is. This will be our fourth Healing Mass in the Cathedral. The first was in 1999 just before the start of the new millennium. It was the third of December, the Mass due to start at 7.30 pm. There was a fierce force seven gale blowing in from the Atlantic, with gusts of icy wind, hail and snow. The Cathedral staff had printed some fifteen-hundred service sheets. They ran out before the Mass started. Twenty-eight priests came that night to help with prayer and the sacrament of reconciliation, which is so central to all healing.

The second Mass was the Friday before Pentecost in the year 2001. It was a fine calm evening, with the June sunlight still shining through the rich colours of the stained glass of the cathedral. That night the Archbishop agreed to be the chief Celebrant. It was a joy for us to have the chief Shepherd of the diocese with us. There were even more people and more priests. That night something extraordinary happened; the action of the Holy Spirit is unpredictable. We do not look for signs and wonders. If they happen we praise God.

The third of these Cathedral Masses was on Sept 8th 2002. It was at 5pm. Again it was a beautiful evening. There was a large police presence because of a hoax phone-call that a bomb had been planted in the Cathedral. The Mass next Friday will be different. They all are. It begins at 7 pm. It looks outward. The healing of Christ also evangelises the believers and the doubters.

24

The Invisible Man

I went into one of those mega stores, huge warehouses full of machinery or food, furniture or electronics They have them in most big industrial estates, they have wiped out the little shops that were so friendly. The bigger the store the less human they become.

The one I went into had a security guard at the door. He was big and he had the cap and the badge. He looked at me suspiciously; at least he looked at me. I smiled, he scowled, as though that was his job. They usually have these welcoming parties at the entrance to these soulless factories.

After wandering around for a while in this big hangar, I found what I wanted and went to the desk, which had "Pay here" written large above it. They have mastered the art of clarity in these matters. A young lady was behind the desk. She was on the telephone. She did not glance at me. Admittedly it is easy to miss me, but I did my best to attract her attention. The phone conversation went on and on. I felt a sudden surge of anger. It was not that I was in a hurry, for I was not. It was because to her I did not exist. But I knew I did exist. I had seen myself in the mirror when I shaved in the morning. I did exist. God knew it, for He made me and He lives in me; it was not, alas, a unique occurrence.

My mind flashed back to another occasion when I had to visit a school… it was 'one of ours.' I was looking for one of the staff who normally was free to see me. The lady at the information desk at the entrance hall of the school was very friendly, and led me to a room that had two doors. They faced each other on opposite sides of the room, which was sparely furnished with a small table and a chair. On the table were odds and ends making a display, and a magazine for the perusal of anyone who was waiting in the room. I remember that I waited a fair length of time while someone searched for the teacher I had arranged to see. During this time teachers passed through the room every few minutes. Not one looked at me, smiled, said "Hello," asked a question. They went through in their spotless white shirts and blouses, carrying books or briefcases. They did not see me. To them I was invisible.

When I left, there was a pupil outside the entrance door. He was awkward, tall and gangling, sitting on a broken chair. I stopped and said "It's going to rain' His face lit up. He mumbled something, and I passed on. There is something crushing about situations like this. G.K Chesterton based one of his detective stories on the phenomenon. In the story the invisible man was the postman. People had become so accustomed to him in the morning that they did not see him. Homeless men, forced to sleep on the streets have sometimes said that the most terrible thing about homelessness is that people do not see them. It is a denial of their humanity. In prison camps prisoners had a number tattooed on their arm. They lost their identity. My total certainty is that God made me, that He made me unique, that 'every hair on my head has been numbered' (though it's easy enough to count them now!). That I am more valued than many sparrows, that I am loved by my Father...... all these certainties make it possible to shrug off these incidents and laugh at them.

But it is not like that with young men and women who do not have my kind of certainty. They also are deeply conscious that they are unique and special, even though society does not seem to see them. In their anger they write their names on the underpasses and walls in every town in the country. "The words of the prophets are written on the subway walls." Every piece of mindless graffiti can be a signal that some child is crying out. "Speak to me. I do exist." Too often they are the children with no father, victims of so-called partners who bring them into the world with no deep commitment to each other, and break away from each other leaving a half-loved child. They drift like ghosts around our cities and end up in the care of probation officers or shut away in juvenile prisons. We deal with a very elemental factor in our very being. God never destroys what He has created. So to be treated as though we do not exist cuts at the very heart of who we are. The importance of a nod, a smile, a word, a glance cannot be overestimated. And I know that sometimes I, also, was too busy to recognise it.

25

That Is Of No Value To The Person Who Has Died

ベ&ベ&ベ&ベ&ベ&

There has been subtle change in the approach to a Requiem, as you know! Requiem means rest. The name was given because the mass for someone deceased was a Mass for their eternal rest. That is: ***That the Soul of the dead person would be given eternal peace in the vision of God.*** The reverse to this is the soul which is not in the Presence of God but is waiting and longing for the Presence of God. That state of the Holy Soul not yet perfect enough to enter the Presence of God but still in a purgative state which can be immeasurably helped by a Mass to be set free has been the accepted view for roughly two thousand years, as attested by inscriptions in the Roman catacombs.

The assumption that everyone who dies goes straight to heaven is not the normal view of a wise person. It can be a delusion. That is of no value to the person who has died; it can deny them the power of the prayers which could be of such great value to them in the state in which they find themselves. A Mass to celebrate the life of a dead person might be soothing the hurt of a surviving relative or friend, but it no act of love for the one who has died. On the contrary it is an act of selfishness.

There lives in the Austrian Tyrol a peasant woman who has all her life prayed and worked for the relief of the souls in purgatory. A journalist listened to her over months talking about her revelations of the state of these souls, and their great longing for understanding of their need for our prayers and sacrifices. The book is startling, and one is not bound to believe all she says, or anything she says, but it is a remarkable book and rings true to Catholic tradition in many ways.

So I want you to be very clear that I come to pray for Margaret, as I did with her just before she died and I gave her final absolution.

She was one of a group of dedicated teachers in the early sixties and into the mid seventies. For the initial ten years they were in the charge of Mr. J. Ireland who was an inspirational head teacher and made an impression on the school, which has lasted up to the present day.

The dedication of this group of teachers was very impressive. It was not only in the classrooms but also outside that they took care of the children. They took them to the summer camps where they shared a common table and communal activities. There were concerts and pantomimes and the building of relationships with parents to form real living communities.

Margaret was a central and very vivacious sharer in all these. A devoted wife and loving mother. She deserves well of many people and I appeal to all to pray for her that she might have eternal rest. Your prayers are never wasted.

The Lord is generous above all things. When we find it hard to pray the Holy Spirit takes our prayers and offers them to the Father, for only the Holy Spirit is at the heart of the Mystery of God. Please, I beg you, pray unceasingly for the holy souls and in their turn they will pray for you.

26

Transparency
ન્ને૬્ને૬્ને૬્ને૬્ને૬્ને૬

It was on one of those hot June days that eliminates any half formed wish that I had caught a plane to go to one of those ugly resorts on some foreign coast, where I would waste money on some tiny hotel room overlooking a burnt up landscape and a beach made of black lava.

I was in a valley in the Yorkshire dales where the grass was green and the stiles were hidden behind bushes and ferns. I was talking with a friend about the Faith of the people, and how it ran like a deep river beneath the apparent secularism of modern Britain. "All we need" said I, "is to tap into it; we need to be more transparent ourselves, especially over plans and finances." "Haven't you seen the detailed accounts that have been recently published?" said my companion. I admitted that I had not; did not know such a thing had happened. He sent me them through the post and they arrived two days later. There they were, open, clear, made simple. I did not understand them. I just about follow the receipt from shopping in Kwik Save.

I found the statistics interesting, the numbers of people at Mass, the number of schools and parishes and the cost of various projects. I began to realise how difficult it must be to have charge of a diocese. In the same postal batch, which contained the Diocesan finances, a friend sent me a group of newsletters from various parishes to which her travels had taken her. I could not help noticing the differences in collections at various parishes. Some collections were over one thousand pounds, and one parish where the collection was £130. That was a parish in North Wales. I suppose these things even out because of the charity that is extended when there is real need.

I know that when I was a parish priest and times were hard in some periods of my long stay, the diocese was very kind because other parishes shared their surplus. But the other thing that struck me was the fact that we Catholics do not take collections too seriously.

The Gospel demands generosity, and St. Paul frequently begged in his letters for support for other parts of the Body of Christ. Yet Jesus told us to take no purse when evangelising, only sandals and one tunic, and no food. It was saying something that is at the heart of the Gospel. The Church is better when it is poor, with few financial resources. When the Church is rich, Faith can run into the sand.

This conflict is real and it has haunted the Catholic Church from the earliest ages. When Francis of Assisi saw a vision of the crucified Jesus who spoke to Francis to re-build the Church, he did two things. One was to strip himself naked and walk out of a courthouse, the other was to become a bricklayer and plasterer of a ruin in the valley below Assisi. Neither of which was what Jesus was really asking of him. But it was a beginning. Within a decade there were seven thousand men wearing brown sackcloth preaching the Gospel in the villages of medieval Europe.

In our own times a tiny Albanian nun left the Loreto Sisters in Calcutta and began to gather the rejects of Indian society, babies, children, men and women, so that they could be wrapped in love before they died. As with St. Francis, within a few years, an army of women wearing the primitive sarong of the Indian poor had moved into the broken towns and empty countryside of the world doing the same thing.

It is difficult to resolve contradictions at the very centre of Christianity except through the power of the Spirit. There is that wonderful writing in the letters of Paul where he writes about Jesus healing the walls of division by nailing them to the Cross. Uniting the extremes in that one stupendous act of love. Maybe transparency is difficult for all of us. No one would wish to have to face the barrage of opposition and the searching questions levelled at top politicians in Parliament. Some of it is unfair and pushed on by daily papers whose editors or journalists are not elected by anyone. A transparency based on fear is a mockery of love. And love and compassion are the very soul of the Body of Christ. I do not think that it always helps to do a meditation on a balance sheet. Yet it can be a very powerful image of the Church in the Modern World.

27

Her Eyes Danced And Sang In The Sunshine

The England of our day struggles with its Christianity. It does not like to mention it, but it is the background of its laws, customs, freedom and culture. It came in with the real Enlightenment sometime in the early Anglo Saxon period and is inextricably built into the texture of English life. It is from this that it has inherited the need for equality, dignity, and freedom of the citizens and the duty of welcoming the stranger and the orphan. Despite our obvious sinfulness we are a baptised country, and it shows. Especially, it shows in contrast with deeply broken and impoverished countries.

During a healing session after one of the Masses, I found myself praying with a young girl. At least, she looked young to me. I am not a good judge of these things, She was dark skinned, not black, but very dark with thick black hair. She was painfully thin and worn, as though she had been though some black trauma that had settled into her soul as well as into her body. It seemed to vibrate through her whole being, like electric tremors triggered by the memories. "What am I praying for?" I murmured to her. "I am praying for asylum in this country," she whispered. "My family has been killed, all except my brother who is hiding in the bush. I managed to escape, a friend found me and travelled with me to England."

I did not even catch the name of the African country she came from. There are any number of them where fanatical Muslim groups try to impose their savage laws on

Christians who flee from them in terror. This is not the will of the all-merciful Allah of the Koran.

I prayed deeply with her for a few moments and then asked one of my female helpers to anoint her with the oil of gladness and console her. I had been meditating for some weeks on the idea of Jesus the Saviour, and realised how profound is baptism which took me out of the realm of the "Prince of this world" as Jesus calls it in the Gospel, into the realm of the Prince of Peace. From darkness into light, from death into life.

This helpless, homeless, penniless woman had stepped ashore into a country where education was free, where justice was as fair as human weakness could make it, where the dream of universal health care was free, available, and offered to the poor and the rich alike, where the homeless were given shelter, and the starving where given food. She had fled from darkness into light, from death into life. Or, had she?

Even as she was talking a group of men and women would have her name on a list either to stay or be sent away. The gift of baptism is the Gift of God, free to all who choose it. God is the Merciful One. We are not. And even as I watched her being anointed I felt a terrible revulsion against the clamour of those who would expel the asylum seekers in case their coming would affect the lives of those 'in the kingdom.'

In the days that followed, the image of the dark skinned woman filled my waking thoughts and became the background of my times of prayer. I wondered had I ever refused to admit the needy stranger, or to baptise a child because of some footling reason stemming from some obscure paragraph in a book of Canon Law. I could not remember any. But what if I had? The parallel between asylum seekers and baptism frightened me.

But the Holy Spirit intervened in a curious way. I was coming back from Ireland on the Sea-cat after a three-day visit to a small town outside Longford. The Sea-cat was moving across the gentle swell of the Irish Sea at a smooth forty miles an hour. It was like a panther in full flight. The June sun was creating rainbows from the spray and in the shelter of the top deck the breeze was gentle. One of the 'travelling people' (as they are commonly called) was showing two of his little girls the turbulent white trace of the speeding boat on the blue of the sea. He was a handsome figure of a man, as so many of them are, and the children were dressed in white clothing and with their bushy hair and unrestricted movement they formed a picture of vivid life and freedom.

The man saw me, and he knew me. He picked up one of the little girls in his arms. "This is Bridget," he said, "You baptised her." I looked at the child and her eyes danced and sang in the sunshine.

28

That Christianity Has Not Made The Impact Is Due To Our Failure To Live It

There was a Dutch Dominican, a learned and well-travelled man, of many talents including music, languages, theology, psychology and catechetics, who came to stay with me year after year.

Some of his sayings have always stayed with me, and one of them was this: "You can tell the standard of poverty or riches in any city by its shops." He used to look at jewellers shops particularly to see if they sold junk or real jewels. He seemed to know the difference, although he had nothing himself. He also applied it to bookshops. One could tell the general level of education in a city by the kinds of books in the bookshops; not only that, you could tell the outlook, interests, leisure pursuits of the people in the same way. He applied it to clothes shops, and the quality of cloth. I suppose it is common sense - by their suits you will know them.

So I ended up in Waterstones last week, being the biggest bookstore in my nearest city, and vaguely I was looking for something on New Age. I went to the spacious bookcase which dealt with such subjects and found no book which did. The bookcase was so arranged that the shelves on eye level (not mine, the average!) were all about magic, witchcraft, white witches, black witches, how to cast spells, how to make spells in your own backyard, what ingredients you need for the pot, helpful incantations and so on. I was the only one browsing in the area. All I was lacking was one of the hats from the nearest road works on a motorway.

The subject was next to the children's department, if that means anything to you. Ultimately I found a book, which in a vague way answered my needs, and I bought it. There is very little in the big bookstore which deals with Christianity, and it is difficult to find it. I do not hold this against them because St. Paul's bookshop holds a rich treasury of those books and it is not far away. Nor do I think that the plethora of these books means any more than a keen interest in Harry Potter, which is possibly why it is near the children's books. Nor would I expect it to result in anyone seeing people with nothing on except a pointed hat, dancing around a fire at midnight in the centre of Switch Island.

But it does signify something, something that points to a failure on the part of Christianity to make impact on the consciousness of this generation in our country. When the Christian Faith fades away from the centre of life, the people turn to other things, because we know, instinctively at the very centre of our being, that we are not self-sufficient and we look for help from some other source. We do this despite the assurance of the scientists or the psychologists that we do not need any other source, that we are actually self-sufficient. But, despite all their promptings, we know we are not. In fact, if we thought we were we would be unbearable, arrogant, selfish, domineering, and if we had power from money or status, we could strut the world stage like the world criminals who emerged out of Europe, South America, the Middle East, Africa, Asia and China in the last one hundred years, the latest of whom has just fled from Iraq.

That Christianity has not made the impact is due to our failure to live it. It was not the failure of the doctrine or a diminution of the power of the Holy Spirit. So in the last weeks I have talked to people who once were dedicated to the practice of the Faith, and who have told me with some sorrow that they have left to join other communities. They said that they found no comfort in continuing. They found no love in the dwindling groups at Mass, no welcome when they came in to the church, no greetings when they left, no inspiration in the liturgy or the homilies. On the contrary, the group they joined was inspirational, welcoming, knew their names and welcomed them. They found the word of God was reverenced and explained and the music uplifting. They miss the Blessed Sacrament and the mention of our Lady.

I would say that people like this are exceptional and most of those who leave have never really been committed from their childhood and less still in adolescence. They just become part of the secular scene. But in the hearts of all the longing remains, buried, but insistent.

29

I Was Too Young To Disobey

The years of the Second World War have passed into the distant past, some sixty years down the line and wreathed in mist. But to those who passed through them they still stand out as six extraordinary years in their lifetime. That generation is dying out but the memory of those days remains fresh in people's minds.

My first months as a priest, in the autumn of 1942, were spent in Ashton-in-Makerfield. It was a small town dominated by coal mining and a large Mill. What the Mill turned out I do not know; I was never inside it to see. Smoke from countless small homes and cottages rose into the still winter air. The rough pavements broken by the constant wear of steel tipped clogs made walking perilous, made more so when the frost came.

There were three of us in the house: the Canon, who was the presiding genius of the parish, Father Michael "He walked tall" Casey, and poor little me, a raw immature novice. The parish, which was a large one, was divided into two areas, and Fr. Casey looked after one and I was asked to look after the other. This meant knocking on innumerable doors to become familiar with the families and making the necessary information into some kind of a pastoral programme.

It was one of the few parishes in the Archdiocese where the men were not in the armed forces. Mining was top priority. The armed forces would not accept miners. They were needed in the pits, I was surprised that people were glad to see me and make me welcome and open up their minds to me. But that happened and it blew me sideways at first. It was strenuous and absorbing; and left little time for leisure.

It happened that after some months, Father Casey went away for the inside of a week. And while he was away, in emergency cases, I looked after both areas of the parish.

So it happened that one evening I found a note on the mat asking a priest to go to a certain house and the house was in Fr. Casey's patch. I put on my trilby and got on the bike. It was dark in the street. There were no lights anywhere. Every window was blacked out. The streets were canyons of darkness.

I found the number in the dim light of a pocket torch. A woman showed me up to a bedroom. In the bed was a young woman. Her face was flushed, she was semi-conscious, the bedclothes were in disarray. I covered her up, gently. The older woman who had let me in came up the stairs and entered the room. "The doctor has been and he does not like the way she looks," the woman announced tersely. There was a coal fire in the hearth, a gas lamp hissed and cast a pool of yellow light on the counterpane. I crossed around the bed and took the older woman aside. "What's her sickness?" I asked. The woman hesitated. "It's a complaint that women get," she said. I felt the weight of my inexperience. "Do you want me to bring her Holy Communion?" I asked. "That would be nice," she said. "I could hear her Confession at the same time," I ventured. The woman said again "That would be nice." I was not sure that she knew what I meant.

I cycled back to the house through the night, cycling by starlight. The 'old man' met me coming in. "You've had a sick call?" he queried. I said "yes," and followed him into his sitting room. I told him the address, and that I was not certain of the name. He looked at me. "Don't go back there." He said. "But, Canon, I have promised to bring her communion and hear her confession.." "No" he said. "Leave it." Three days later the undertaker phoned. The girl was dead. Later that day the woman who had let me in called to the house and I met her. I did not tell her that the Canon had forbidden me to go back. "I rang and rang at the door," she said, "when you did not turn up, but nobody answered. I knocked and knocked but no one answered. I tried the doorbell. It was working." "I don't understand," I said. "I was in, and I have very good hearing. So has the housekeeper."

That weekend Fr. Casey came back, and I asked him what it was all about. He took me into his room and closed the door. "She had an abortion. It went wrong. Only back street abortionists will do it." I have never forgotten her; I was too young to disobey. But to this day I pray for her.

30

Resignation

❧❧❧❧❧❧❧❧❧❧❧

It was early evening when I reached the farmhouse standing out over the village in Donegal, but already the darkness had set in.

It was late December. In Letterkenny the Christmas lights were advertising, in the way the secular world does, that it was Advent, meaning "shop now, before Christmas catches you out." I had come over at this time to visit a sick friend. He had multiple cancer. His young wife, distraught at the onset of a deadly sickness in one so comparatively young, had written to me urgently. "Please come over and pray with him." A priest friend was driving me, it was wild mountainous country and beyond my power to drive at night or in strange territory.

The door of the house was open, my friend lifted the latch and went in. "God bless all here" he said, and I found myself in the large kitchen of the house. There was a coal and wood rue burning in the wide hearth, sending heat and the pleasant scent of burning wood into the spacious room. A tall woman came across the room and embraced us. She had the dark hair and gentle eyes of the women of the West, "I'm so grateful," she said.

The patient was sitting in an armchair and I looked at him. He had a full head of brown hair, his eyes were alive, full of humour and intelligence. I asked him about his illness. He told me briefly of the spread of the cancer from his liver to his lungs and now into his spinal cord. He knew what he was talking about for he was a doctor and had a large practice in the surrounding countryside.

We talked about my journey and he asked something about the healing movement. "It's so different to your work," I said, "You use all the knowledge you have gained from the years in medical school, and the experience of medicine in the practice. You apply all that acquired skill and experience to heal your patients. It is different for me - I have to be empty and not depend on anything but the power of the Holy Spirit. If I had the gifts of medical knowledge and the knowledge of psychology or psychiatry, I would have to give up any dependence on them."

"I must not get in the way and obstruct the power of the Holy Spirit, I must be like an empty syringe or an empty saline drip waiting for the Holy Spirit to fill me." He was listening intensely. His wife intervened. "What happens? How do we cooperate?" "It is not easy to answer that question," I said, "Jesus never takes away freedom. Remember the case of the blind man by the wayside. After his demands to go to Jesus were at last met, and they brought him to Jesus, Jesus said, "What do you want me to do?" *(You'd think it was obvious, the man was blind!)* "Oh master, that I might see." Then He gave him back his sight. This is how Jesus works; He never takes away freedom." "But surely!" interposed the woman "it must be clear what a sick person wants?"

Suddenly I was aware of tension in the room. The firelight flickered in the hearth, there was silence for a moment and it seemed to hang in the air. I looked intently at the doctor. There was something about him, a sense of deep peace like a quiescence in the centre of his pain. "It's not that easy" I said. "I had a woman in a wheelchair the other day. She was in constant pain. I asked her what she wanted Jesus to do for her. She said, "I want my grandchild to be baptised." It was her choice. I knew that if she had asked to be healed, she might be walking today."

Then the doctor spoke. "I was a long time out of the Church, I pursued medicine with a hunger for knowledge, I wanted success and nothing else mattered. I left Faith hanging on a hook fashioned in childhood. It just hung there and I noticed it and left it hanging. When I found out I had cancer and that it was terminal, I entered into the mystery of Faith again and was reconciled."

He smiled. "I went to Mass and Communion one evening in the church near where my surgery is, in town. Half the people there were my patients. They thought I was a non-Catholic before that. They just gathered around me; it was very moving." He paused, then he said "Something happened later that week which I cannot describe." I looked deeply into his eyes and I think I knew. I began to pray for him. I prayed for his healing and I prayed for his peace. Silently I prayed for the beautiful woman who loved him more than her own life. I finished, exhausted.

Driving back through the night the priest said to me. "What do you think?" "I don't know!" I said. "He may have had a glimpse of a light and a beauty that is incomprehensible and he may not want to turn back."

31

The Call

People who were at the Cathedral on the afternoon and evening of Sunday 17th August will know that a team from Kerala, India, were conducting an unusual service in that hallowed spot. There were two priests by the name of Matthew, one sixty-seven years old, one forty-four. The senior Father Matthew was the superior; he was also the founder of the Potta Ministry, which attracts something like 30,000 retreatants a day to the remote part of Kerala named Potta.

I was asked to play a small part in their mission and did so not only in Liverpool, but also in Newcastle, Manchester and Birmingham. It was because of this that I learned something about the nature of their apostolate and also something about the men themselves. The senior member Father Matthew, some time after his ordination to the priesthood, had a powerful experience of the coming of the Holy Spirit which he called a second baptism or baptism in the Spirit. It affected his body and soul, like flames of fire passing through and around him. It was followed by an inner voice speaking to him, asking him to begin the work he does now.

Mr Myles Dempsey, founder of the Prince of Peace Community, has spoken about a similar experience after which he began the Conference "New Dawn at Walsingham" and "New Dawn in Ireland." Mother Teresa of Calcutta spoke about a similar experience while on a railway train on her way to Darjeeling, telling her to leave the Loreto convent and go out to the poor. There must be, I know, many similar interventions by God in history, the outstanding example being what happened to St. Paul on the road to Damascus. But what do you do when people start coming to you and saying that they also are hearing the Voice of God telling them to do something?

When I was very young priest I used to encourage people to think again. But I had no right to do that. I must listen to them carefully and try to help them to see whether it is real or not. For why shouldn't the Holy Spirit, or the Blessed Virgin, or Padre Pio or any other saint speak with God's permission to Johnny Todd or Mary Pugwash? And what's the good of the Communion of Saints if it does not include it?

Some years ago a lady used to come to Mass every day and receive Holy Communion, then go home to an empty little flat with the minimum of furniture and a larder which only held tins of baked beans and some bread. She was married and had three children. Her husband had left her. The three young schoolboys lived on the beans and bread. She said that she had been told to live only on the Blessed Sacrament. She was still young. Her body was painfully thin and she seemed to be transparent after we received the Body of Christ.

As the boys grew they became very troublesome; they played truant and stole food. One of them was taken to a Young Offenders' Unit. They were treated with great kindness in the Junior School; the Head teacher gave them food instead of punishing them. I told the lady that God would not give her the gift of children and make it impossible for her to feed and look after them. She said I was wrong and that she had to obey the inspiration of the

Holy Spirit. She consulted a theologian who specialised in Mystical Theology. He told me he was convinced that her case was genuine. She was always joyful and gentle. It was all very mysterious, the medical doctors were baffled by it all. Years later the boys, now young men, gave up all Faith in God and scattered to live abroad. Before this she was taken to a psychiatric unit and spent most of the rest of her life there.

Some three years before she died she was released and I resumed seeing her. To this day I do not know who was right about her. The only certainty I have is that she is in heaven. But the gift of discernment is a special gift; we need people who have a gift like that from the Holy Spirit to perceive, first of all, whether the condition is medical or spiritual. So we don't make the mistake made by the police and medicos, one hundred and forty five years ago, of trying to lock up a young girl they thought was a mentally disturbed menace, until the day she knocked on the door of the baffled and battered priest and said to him "The lady said, 'I am the Immaculate Conception'."

32

The Artist

In the cool of the evening of one of those very hot summer days which still linger in our memories, I sat in a garden on the outskirts of Maastricht, the ancient Roman town in which Margaret Thatcher signed the treaty which brought the European Union into being. There were four of us on a patio surrounded by foliage. Lamps hung from trees illuminating a small swimming pool, the scent of cabbages, sprouts and turnips came to us from the large field at the end of the garden where Holland merged into Belgium.

It was the home of Leonard, in his mid thirties, medium height, very gentle, with dark wavy hair. He had created the garden, and filled the house, which led to the garden, with his paintings and other creations. The house was a curious blend of comfort and small art gallery, with a dark wood piano in the background. The other two in the garden were women, one old and one young. We talked about the ethical problems of the failing Church, as people in Holland tend to do when they sit in gardens with cups of coffee in front of them. Needless to say, our views differed but it did not seem to matter too much on this blissful evening in a magic garden.

Later, the friend who introduced me to Leonard gave me more details about him, She admired him and liked him. He had been a big help to her, and she to him. They are good neighbours. Now all this has little to do with the Catholic Pictorial, but for the fact that wherever you go in Western

Europe you are confronted with the presence of the Catholic Church.

It is different to England; the difference is the Catholic Faith. I say this despite the fact that Holland is not a good example of living Catholicism. Yet off the main square of this ancient and beautiful town at the crossing of the river Meuse (Maastricht), in the place where the people drink at café tables surrounded by trees, and medieval buildings, there is the shrine of Our Lady Star of the Sea, before which a thousand candles burn day by day. People, young, old, and children, kneel and pray for a few moments then pass on their way. The shrine is open to the street. They have done this as long as records have been kept, and they do it to this day and still say "I don't believe" although they do.

That was also England before the so-called Reformation, which closed the door firmly on all this beauty. It seems to me, in the way an out-of-date geriatric might see our world, that behind the antipathy to Europe and the Euro and all that goes with it, is the deep-rooted fear and dislike produced by centuries of anti-Catholicism, now still insinuated by the media and the BBC

A short time later I wandered into the town of Tongeren in Belgium and once again settled down in the shaded square of the town at a table to drink an ice cold coca cola. Belgium is different again from Holland. Anyone of ripe age can travel anywhere in Belgium by train or bus for the irresistible price of two euro fifty. This gift is due to the persistence of a socialist Minister for Transport. Naturally I claimed my share of the transport and must admit that their railways are very good.

In the fourth century Tongeren was the Roman capital of this part of the Low Countries. In this town square is the fearsome statue of the last great Gallic warrior who fought the Romans to liberate the country. As I was admiring it a man approached me and made himself known. He had met me on a previous occasion and we had exchanged cards. This time he took me to his home. To my surprise it was similar to the house in Maastricht. It was an artists' home, full of paintings and objects of art. It was then he told me that he had met Leonard when he was a patient in hospital... suffering from a deep depression. His profession is to use art and sculpture as a therapy for such disorders. It was under his tutelage that Leonard had been liberated and found the gift of artistic expression. His work is deeply religious. He evangelises. But not in the way we do, for indeed, there are many pathways to Christ.

33

The Tramp
⊰⊱⊰⊱⊰⊱⊰⊱⊰⊱

It is approximately forty-four years since Canon Stephens died in the Providence Hospital, St. Helens. He was born towards the end of the nineteenth century in Woolton, which at that time was a small village some miles outside Liverpool.

The lovely church which stands on high ground overlooking the village street was in the care of the Benedictine's, and their love for liturgy and the atmosphere of peace which characterised their demeanour was attractive to the young Edward; he longed to join them. But it was not to be and he was sent to Ushaw for studies for the priesthood.

At this time the building of Upholland was only at the discussion stage. Ushaw was to be his home for very many years. He told me of his first term when his case was taken to the train in Liverpool, and he took a stagecoach from Durham to Ushaw. And 'Stagecoach' was not the trade name for a bus company. It was the genuine article you see on Christmas cards surrounded by snow and holly.

Ushaw Moor was bleak and cold, and so was the college. He suffered but survived. His first appointment after his ordination was to the Cathedral at Lancaster, which at that time was part of the Diocese of Liverpool.

It was while he was there that something happened which was to become a legend. One of the priests, whether it was in the Cathedral or some other parish church I do not know, was called in the middle of the night by loud knocking on the door. A tall man in riding leathers was holding a panting horse by the bridle. He asked the priest to come with him to a sick man on the moors. The stranger was holding a lantern in one hand and his speech was courteous. The priest asked his name, but the stranger simply said, "I am a friend of the sick man and time is pressing."

The priest felt insecure but realised that he had to take the risk. He went inside and dressed for the journey, took the pyx with the Blessed Sacrament and the Holy Oils for the anointing. It was the late nineteenth century; whether he had his own horse or the stranger took him on his I could not remember, but somehow he and the stranger went in the darkness to the bleak moors which run from the dark peat of Blackstone Edge to the wilderness of Cam Fell.

There in a ruined stone house he found a man dying by an empty fireside. He asked the stranger to leave while he knelt by the man and heard his confession. The man was an Irishman who had come to work in England. He was ragged and dirty, but the priest was overwhelmed by the obvious holiness of the man. He received viaticum with reverence and love. The priest left him as the dawn was breaking. He asked the man who was the strange horseman. By this time he had vanished. The dying man was surprised. "There is nobody that knows me," he said, "No one has come near me."

Some days later the newspaper in Lancaster had a short note to say that a shepherd had found a corpse in an empty house high up on the moors. He was an unknown tramp and they buried him in a pauper's grave. I was assistant priest in Birkdale during the time he was parish priest there. He told me this more or less as I have written it while I was with him; he repeated it to me many times as he reached old age.

It obviously had left a deep impression on him and he had no doubt that the stranger on the horse was indeed the man's guardian angel.

I had the impression that it took place while he was young priest in Lancaster, but I may be mistaken about that. He left the Cathedral in Lancaster to become a teacher of classics at Ushaw, and eventually became the Headmaster of the Lower School, presiding over studies for the young students up to the age of eighteen. He was held in some awe and admiration for his learning and his piety. He left there just before the beginning of the Second World War and was appointed to St. Patrick's, Newton le Willows, and thence to Birkdale.

I learned a great deal from him, simply because of who he was, and some of his learning rubbed off on me, but not a lot, and much as I admired and tried to imitate his piety, I have to admit, it was bridge too far.

◇ ◇ ◇ ◇ ◇ ◇

Love Not Thyself.
Love not thyself, for then life closes in.
To such a narrow space, your heart within.

Love all without, if you would seek true peace.
Forget yourself. Let restless yearnings cease.

Follow the saints, who really gave their all
And answered "me Lord" to their Saviour's call.

P. Williams 2005

34

The Power Of Prayer
❦❦❦❦❦❦❦❦❦❦❦

In August I had the privilege of being with a group of gifted and holy Indian priests who had come to England to lead people in Faith and prayer. In the course of this they came also to our Cathedral.

It was not easy to understand the way the Indian priests from the Potta Ministry of Kerala carried out the healing ministry. The talks were long, punctuated with Alleluia and 'Blessed be God.' The content of the talks was all based on Scripture quotations from different parts of the Bible, from Genesis to Revelations. The speakers went up and down the Bible as though it were a keyboard. They halted frequently to announce that certain ailments were being healed.

There were four in the team. The leader was Fr. Matthew. They were holy and ascetical. It was just not the way we do things. But they had an air of certainty about them, after all the experience of some thirty thousand per day at Potta has taught them more than I could ever learn. They said to me that the proclamation of the Word was what Jesus had told the apostles to do, that after the proclamation of the Word the signs and wonders would inevitably follow.

I was in Alsager in Cheshire four weeks later. A lady met me and said she had been born with a defect in one leg. It left her with one leg shorter than the other. The limp had led to damage in the hip. The result was constant pain and the onset of arthritis. She had gone to the service in our Cathedral. The next morning both legs were the same length and all her pain had gone. She had seen her G.P then the Consultant, and they just said it was beyond them "Go home and enjoy life."

The Beatles in the '70's used to visit India to be guided by a Guru. It led to a fashion to look to India for mysticism and wisdom. One of the great Indian teachers, Fr. Rufus Pereira who loves his native India, does not like all the aspects of Hinduism and some of its satellite teachings. "I have been led to believe," he wrote "that many of these gods and goddesses in Hindu mythology are nothing other than demons." He warned us against the use of transcendental meditation and certain other practices which had entered into Western Christianity. You have to take seriously a person of his stature.

The prayer of Christians is pure and untarnished, based on the Gospel and the adoration of the Holy Trinity. We all know the power of prayer, we have immense spiritual resources if we use them. I must admit that it is only in the last fifteen years that I have been praying with people in contrast to praying for them. And by 'praying with' people I do not mean saying the formal prayers, which have been sanctified by centuries of use, prayers like the Our Father and the Hail Mary.

By praying with people I mean answering their particular need. For instance if someone has a headache or has asthma I will pray while I am with them that they may be healed of their sickness. So I pray for the headache to go. Sometimes in doing this, I am made aware of an underlying cause for the headache and begin to pray that the situation in the home might change and that people will forgive each other, or something else if that arises. This effect on people is heightened if other people join me in praying for some such intention.

The union of others in a prayer is always helpful. In the same way if there is a problem in the community it is possible to unite in prayer for that. For example, some time ago a prayer group in London, a very powerful prayer group meeting in Soho, became sickened by the spread of sex shops and pornography visibly on sale in the area.

For some weeks they united in prayer against the sponsors of the degradation. One by one the sex shops closed and the lurid advertisements went out. Using prayer power it is possible to alter most things.

Early in 1950 a serving officer in the army, a professed agnostic, came to me and asked it I could do anything for his wife who was seriously ill. She was convinced that she was in hell. There were four young children in the house, which was badly kept, as were the children. He had taken her to many counsellors and some psychiatrists, but without effect. I asked a group of Legionaries of Mary to say the rosary every day in the house. The woman recovered and the children were baptised. The agnostic recognised the power and was astonished, but he had not changed. In it is what Jesus promised if we have faith, even as small as a mustard seed! But do we have that kind of Faith, and do we have people who use it?

35

Can We Share This Dream

It was a nurse who came to see me, a children's nurse, a children's nurse who worked in schools.

She was tall and slender, black hair and black boots, with eyes filled with enthusiasm and a face which was placid from a joy which came from deep within her, the rare gift of the Holy Spirit.

She came for a blessing on a unique project which she had been working on for some years. The origin of it lay in her growing experience of children suffering from ill health and being sick because of stresses coming from living in families which were broken, or lonely, or filled with anger.

The sickness was different from the sickness coming from malnutrition or deep poverty because, strangely, under-nourished children from these families showed none of the above symptoms. As if to make up for their hunger, they were loved and cherished, in the care of parents who loved each other.

She told me about her own experience, of the years when Faith was dimmed by a growing atmosphere of spiritual apathy in her home, the schools, and the inevitable drift away from prayer. She had an awakening and began to try again. She found a new way of prayer in Carmelite spirituality and the writings of John Main.

This led her into the prayer of silence and a growing love for the words of Scripture and the book by that unknown Medieval English mystic who wrote "The Cloud of Unknowing." Her inner life changed and she found herself with an abiding peace. This is what she longed to give to the innocent victims of stress.

From this vision, with which she had wrestled with for years, she produced a remarkable work which she brought to me for a blessing. The object is to bring calmness and stillness into the classroom, by bringing this type of contemplative prayer into the lives of children on a daily basis. She tried it, and it worked.

She has patented the course, and is currently endeavouring to have it entered into the school day across the whole education programme. The group she is using it for are the year group leaving Junior school and the year group entering secondary education. For it to secure general acceptance, she has avoided making it clearly Christian which it actually is.

When I was twelve or thirteen, prayer was always an activity bound by stern rules. I had to do it every day, night and morning. I threw words at God who I hoped was listening. I knew that Jesus was God, so most of the words were said to Him. They were of two kinds, the things I wanted, like passing an exam or a place in the football team, and things I was taught to say in formulas like the Our Father and Hail Mary.

I did not always understand the formulas. Words like "Blessed is the fruit of thy womb" were a puzzle. I did not know what a womb was, nor how I could call Jesus "fruit." But I said them anyway. The one called then The Holy Ghost, was really a ghost. There was something creepy about Him, I avoided Him, but had to bring Him into it because He always got a honourable mention.

I liked day dreaming, darkness and light, the Christmas tree, the comfortable feeling at Mass. Candles, music, the presence of love and friendship. The fact that I could find God in the depth of things like these was never considered. The idea of total silence, listening to Him, awareness of beauty, of a Presence, never entered into my instruction.

If I told a priest that I had spent prayer time like that, the chances were that he would say I was giving in to distractions. But I wasn't. Only in maturity did prayer move into different channels and that was the work of the Holy Spirit. But I did not know Him at that time. That secret of inner peace which comes from such prayer, that abolishes stress and anxiety, is a gift which changes life. The idea, the vision that this could be introduced into the lives of children at an early age via the education system of our country is staggering. Only God knows what result could flow from it.

When the history of the re-evangelisation of our country comes to be written it might well be that the work of a simple Catholic school nurse could stand as an important factor in the prayer life of the people.

36

Our Man In Rome Meets Teresa's People
ન૭ન૭ન૭ન૭ન૭ન૭

I was in Rome to see Mother Teresa beatified. The last time I was there was to see Liverpool win the European cup, so this was different.

I took the Metro from the Spanish Steps. A train rumbles in every few minutes, daubed with graffiti, like they used to be on the Manhattan subways, and packed unbelievably. I was squeezed in like a tangerine squashed between hot breathing bodies, out of reach of the vertical steel bars, and too small to reach the overhead one, which the others clung to. It stopped at St Pietro, spewed us out on to the platform and vanished down a tunnel. I had a ticket, gift of the Missionaries of Charity, enabling me to act as a Minister of the Holy Eucharist. There was a note printed on the bottom of the ticket advising me to check in to the Chiesa di San Lorenzo. I had tried without success the day before to find out where this church of San Lorenzo was, but no one seemed to know.

Now it was the day itself, the Mass was due to start at 10 am, but it was only 7.30. I felt I had time.

St Peter's Square was already full, barriers everywhere and endless officials. Some were tall men dressed as though they had stepped out of a set from the Godfather, but with little plastic badges to notify that they were important. There were Swiss Guards, tall and magnificent, nonchalant, unemotional. Police of various degrees, guides and workers in red or yellow plastic. Every few yards a barrier manned by one of these. Behind the barriers was the world, the patient waiting world of women, children, young men and old men. I stopped at every barrier and showed the card.

"San Lorenzo!" Swiss Guards, police, workers, no-one had heard of San Lorenzo. I was desperate.

I saw a crowd of young men dressed in cassocks, carrying surplices. They were still black haired like we all were once. I skipped through a barrier, bunked in and joined them. I put on my alb and stole to look authentic and sat down. The student next to me was reading something in English. He told me that the groups were Legionaries of Christ. I told him that one of my young men from Kirkby had joined them some years ago.

The student knew him and admired him. He told his friends on the adjacent chairs and I was in. It was cold waiting, bitterly cold. I froze slowly. Over the loud speakers the speaker read out quotations from Mother Teresa: "The joy of Jesus is the flame of burning love. You cannot have joy without sacrifice."

The time for acting in the Eucharistic Ministry began at the Offertory when a long line of priests went to a sacristy to collect ciboria, already consecrated. And the room where they were waiting had over the doorway "Centre di San Lorenzo." Mystery solved.

Then into the sunshine to begin the distribution of Holy Communion. I was in the wide space between the barriers. A young Legionary of Christ held a white umbrella high above my head. The crowds were wedged tight against the barrier, the pressure from the back pinning people against the wood.

Hands appeared waving in the air. The hands of the black people, the hands of the Asians, the hands of white people.

Hands smooth with youth, hands lined with age or labour. The hands of the hungry for the Bread of Life. It was intensely moving.

I could see faces, anxious in case they might be left out. I began to smile with joy facing the crowd, they began to smile back. Now the sun was shining, and I was so privileged to be feeding the people hungry for this Bread of Eternal Life. They were the people Teresa talked about.

It was over; I was back in the crowd, facing the great Basilica of 'Saints Peter and Paul,' which stands over the tomb of the first Pope. Carved in the stone on the top of the building in large letters "IN HON PRINCIP APOST, PAUL V BURGHESIUS ROMANUS. PONT MAX." So he was a Roman, a member of the Burghesi Family, one of the richest and most powerful families of the 16th century.

On this day, below that proud inscription, in total contrast was the illuminated picture of a little woman from Albania, dressed in a Sari who lived and died with nothing but a love which conquered the world.

37

Would You Take A Ticket Out?

≪≫≪≫≪≫≪≫≪≫≪≫

I was coming out of the church the other day after Mass and met up with a tall young man whom I had never seen before as far as I know.

It was one of those fine crisp autumn days when the sun is shining on the leaves which carpet the ground outside the path from the church and the sun shines hazily through the remaining foliage on the trees. There was a sniff of winter moving in, I had zipped up the collar of the old coat which covered my shrinking bones. The young man was dressed in blue jeans and a jacket, which seemed inadequate in the cool breeze.

I was thinking of a cup of coffee and was on my way to the place where I knew it was on offer. The young man said "It is a nice church." I agreed. "You're not from here?" I asked. "No" he said. He was walking by my side, towering over me. He obviously thought I was one of the group of old people who make up the crowd at morning Masses on weekdays, and of course, I was. But I was wrapped up in an old coat I had bought in Belfast eight years before and I guess he did not know that I was a priest.

"It was cold last night," he said. I agreed. "I slept in the park," he said. Then he added "I've been in prison, and was discharged a short time ago." I gathered, then, that his pious visit to the porch of the church was not entirely based on devotion.

At this point the question to be asked is never "why were you sent to prison?" so I said "it's not easy when you come out." I know that this is a safe statement. By this time we had left the church gate and were walking along the road with the old trees with twisted trunks lining it. They seemed to be listening to the conversation and nodding that they had heard it all before.

He said "I need somewhere to stay. If I had somewhere to stay, the social security would help me. But when I go to them now they tell me that they can't give me any money when I have no address, and no one will give me a place unless I have the money to pay for it."

I knew that this was a true statement. But there are exceptions. I stated one of them. "Have you tried the Sisters in Seel Street?" "Yes," he said, "They took me in and gave me this jersey and jacket. They were good to me. But I could not stand the smell from the winos and the nights in the bedrooms." I could accept that.

The Missionaries of Charity see the rejects of society in a different way. They are Jesus, mocked by the crowd. This lithe young man is not a Missionary of Charity. "What about your family?"

"I grew up in the Old Swan," he answered. "I was baptised in St Oswald's and made my first communion there. I became an altar boy and served on the altar until I was twelve."

"Later I drifted away and got into bad company. I became the black sheep. I lost touch with my brothers. We all broke up."

"Where are your family?" I asked. "There are some living in Liverpool, but they won't see me. There is one sister who keeps in touch and cares, but she lives in London."

"Would she take you in?" He replied: "I think she would. But how can I go to London?

I did not ask him about his father and mother. It was clear that there was a breakdown in relationships. It was evident that the family had tried, received him back time and again, and finally decided that they had to get on with their own lives for everyone has to carry their own burdens. That, also can be the hard lesson that alters the course of life of someone who has been living off their backs. Was this his moment of destiny?

"I will buy you a ticket to London," I said. I don't think he believed me. "How can you? You can't book from here."

"You can" I said. "Will you accept?" We were walking towards the station at this time. The red lights were flashing at the level crossing. A train rolled slowly out of the station and the barriers on the road lifted.

"I will" he said. In the booking office I asked for a single to Euston. I paid by switch card on the principle, ride now, pay later. It was £48. I gave him the ticket and left him on the platform waiting for the next train. I waved to him from the road as he stood there, a forlorn figure in jeans and the clothes from the Missionaries of Charity.

"He'll sell the ticket in Liverpool" said the friend to whom I mentioned the incident. "I don't mind that" I said. "The Lord told me to give it to him. I was not told how he must use it."

38

Do You Reject Satan?
࿎࿎࿎࿎࿎࿎࿎࿎࿎࿎

One Sunday afternoon in the 1990's I had a number of babies to baptise. There was a large crowd in the church. I came to the part where the parents and godparents profess their faith in the teachings of the Church.

I told the people I wanted them, the community to which the children belonged, to join in the profession of Faith. I said, "There are six questions: three negative, three affirmative. I want you all to answer in the name of the children." I began with the first.

"Do you reject Satan?"

"And, please, I want you to answer."

Now there was total silence except for the crying of a baby.

"Do you reject Satan?"

I was using a microphone. There was no answer. Just silence. I repeated. "I need an answer, do you reject Satan?" Again silence. Then a man stood up at the back of the church. "Father," he said "we don't believe in him." I asked the crowd "is that the general feeling?" There was a murmur of assent.

"Alright" I said. "Do you believe in God?"

There was immediate agreement... and so it was for the last two questions of the six, about Jesus, and about the end of the Creed. I baptised the babies.

The man who had spoken was honest, and he was obviously speaking not only for the majority of the group in the church, but probably for the majority of the men who met together in the bars and pubs and football pitches of the town. And even when I was a young student, in those far off days, I wondered about the Gospel read on the first Sunday in Lent, about the encounter of Jesus with Satan in the desert at the end of His forty-day fast.

But no longer! It was not the kind of thing my mind dwelt upon in the early years of my priesthood, but an event occurred in my early years in Southport, which focused my mind on it. It was the time just after the Second World War.

Southport attracted a substantial number of immigrants, refugees from the devastation of Europe. Among them was a young French girl. *(These were the days before communion in the hand.)* She had been going to communion and taking the Sacred Host out of her mouth, wrapping it in tissue, and carrying it out of the church. She was doing it under orders of someone she called 'Le Pasteur.' She had met him in Domremy with a group of young English followers. She had been attracted by their courtesy and kindness and had accepted an invitation from them to join them in Southport. They had secured her a job as an au pair girl in a big house near our presbytery. She was tormented by guilt.

"What did they do with the Sacred Host?" I asked. She told me, halting in fear, talking in her quaint French. "There was circle, a low, round stone table, a ceremony." I did not press her. "Do you want to leave them?" She did, but she was terror-stricken. They had threatened to strike her in some way if she ever betrayed them or left the group. She gave me permission to repeat what she had told me. But Le Pasteur must not know, or any of the group. Nor did she reveal where they lived or where it all took place.

Next morning I went to the Police Station in Lord Street, Southport. I asked to see the sergeant. The man at the desk asked me what it was for. I refused to discuss it, and probably, because I was a priest, he agreed to call down the sergeant.

The big man came down the stairs, took me into a side room and sat me down. I told him about the encounter. He took notes. I could see he was out of his depth. 'I was a nut case,' was written all over his face, but possibly not on his note pad. I did not comment on his looks. He could have eaten me in one bite He showed me politely to the door. I thought I was singing against the wind.

Two days later the phone rang. It was the Chief of Police. He wanted to see me and his manner was vastly different. He took it very seriously. He said he would put a plain-clothes policewoman to cover the house where the girl was working. The policewoman would discreetly follow her to try and find out the place where this happened, because the group met once a week. That week the girl never once left the house. The policewoman was withdrawn.

That very evening the girl went out and met the group. Finally I persuaded her to renounce Satan, break the solemn pact she had sworn, renew her Faith and dedication to Jesus and the Church. I gave her absolution and Holy Communion. She fled back to France. Months later she wrote to me from a sanatorium near Paris. She had suffered from a large tumour since she left England. In her letter, she thanked God for saving her.

It is fifty or more years ago since that happened and I have never heard from her since. But, if she is still alive, she will understand something about the power of the Christ who met Satan in the desert. And if she brought her children for baptism and the French priest said, "Do you reject Satan?" She would certainly not say. "We don't believe in him?"

39

She Held Us All Spellbound
⚜⚜⚜⚜⚜⚜

Being retired has its advantages. After the ecstasy of the Beatification of Mother Teresa in Rome, the wisdom that flowed from all that experience, I left the perpetual noise and struggle of Rome's pavements for the quiet solitude of the West of Ireland.

It was a bank holiday weekend in the Republic. The sun was shining, the skies were blue, it was warmer than Rome, and the Atlantic Ocean was moving against the cliffs of the island with majestic calmness.

High up on those cliffs is the last farm before America, called the Southernmost Farm. With a huge fire lit in the ancient hearth, it was the setting for a storytelling workshop 2003.

The Master storyteller was a lady by the name of Dovie Thomason. She is an award-winning storyteller, recording artist and author. She has shared tales at the Globe Theatre, on the BBC, at youth conflict resolution projects in Northern Ireland, tribal pow-wows and festival stages world-wide. She is a full-blooded Apache Indian and tells stories heard since childhood, shared with her Lakota and Apache relatives.

I saw her sitting in a rocking chair by the fire. I had not seen a face like hers since the last Cowboy v Indian film on the Gaumont. In fact it brought me back to my boyhood fixation about Tom Mix, where I saw that face in black and white films. She had long black hair and an inscrutable visage, ageless and unemotional. It was only when she looked into my eyes that I saw things I had not seen before. Down to her ankles she was dressed in black, with a little grey cloak on her shoulders.

The stories she told were about animals and prairies and birds and sunshine and snow. There was a quality of legend in them. They had been polished by centuries of telling around fires in the woodlands, by lakes, at the foot of deep mountains and woods too dense to penetrate. Her chief had to agree that she could tell the stories. She was not allowed to tell the ones that were sacred and confined only to the tribes. She held us spellbound.

At the heart of the American Indian oral tradition is a deep and unconditional belief in the efficacy of language. Words are intrinsically powerful. They are magical. By means of words many things can happen. Perhaps the most distinctive and important aspect of their tradition is their respect for a belief in language. Words are spoken with great care, and they are heard. They must be taken seriously. To be careless in the presence of words, on the inside of language, is to violate a fundamental morality. I found it all absorbing.

When she told the stories her whole being seemed to come alive and all her body and mind took part in it. There were twenty-four people at the sessions, some from Canada, some from Ulster, from Scotland, Israel, the West of Ireland, and the United States. Obviously we all shared in the workshops and told stories from our own heritage. But there are many lessons to be learnt.

The overall impression in my mind was that nowhere in history is there a story that even remotely approaches the story of a God entering the world through a young girl in Nazareth, and that the One called "The Word" by St John in his Gospel, was made known by the faint sound of the beating of an infant heart in the silence of Mary's womb. But of that extraordinary story and the multitudinous legends, poetry, art and music of the Christian story, which followed that, the Apache woman did not speak.

She had not come for that; on my part I was glad to be given some insight into the centuries old culture that existed among the Indians who inhabited America before the coming of the Pilgrim Fathers.

The sun was shining on the heather and the cliffs, the sea birds were wheeling against the blue of the sky, in the evenings the pubs were alive with music and laughter. It was good to be back on the neighbouring island, nearer to the mainland, where my mother was born and spent her childhood. I had been there when people smoking clay pipes told the stories of the past and sang the songs.

But they were different stories and different songs, and old as I am, I still hear them.

40

'*I Knew Then He Still Loved Me*'
&ɔ&ɔ&ɔ&ɔ&ɔ&ɔ

The weekend before Christmas I was the guest of a group staying at Wistaston Hall, which is an ancient seventeenth century manor house on the outskirts of Crewe. These days it is a retreat house of the Oblates of Mary Immaculate.

Crewe was one of those small country towns raised to national importance by the railways. It was, and is, a centre of a confluence of railway lines. There is something about the loneliness of a railway station, scene of heartbreaking farewells, especially in wartime; it was brought home to me because of an experience of my sister.

Early in the year 1939 she booked a passage on a liner sailing from Liverpool to Boston, in order to have the dream holiday of her life. By 1939 she had been teaching for some years and our cousins in Boston were constantly inviting her to visit them. The imminence of war was rarely mentioned in the news of the day. The war broke out while she was there. Our cousins invited her to stay in America and take up a teaching post there. What was to have been a four-week holiday became six months.

Meanwhile she had met a young American in Boston and they began to go out together. He was a Catholic; they went to Mass together and called to each other's homes. In December of 1939 she decided to return to wartime England and sailed in a convoy from New York to Liverpool before Christmas. She resumed her teaching post, and began a voluminous correspondence with her friends in Boston.

The flow of letters lessened when America entered the war in 1941. Then she received word that her friend was now in the American army and was en-route for Britain. He communicated with her from various parts of the country where they were in training. In war time no-one in the armed forces could indicate where they were.

She gathered from phone calls that some of the time he was in Scotland. Towards the end of May 1944 he phoned her. It was a cryptic message. The content was something like "I have to ask you a question of deep importance to both of us, and if you give the kind of answer I hope for, I want to give you something. We are on our way from my present location to somewhere else. I will be staying the night in Crewe. Can you meet me at the hotel?"

It was shortly before D-Day. He was preparing for the invasion of Normandy. He did not mention the name of the hotel because he would not know it. She talked it over with my parents.

On a Friday evening, at the end of a school day, my father saw her to Lime Street Station, and trembling with excitement and expectation, she took the train to Crewe. The town was crowded with American troops. It was night. He had said it would be late when they arrived. She went to the first hotel she saw. The foyer was difficult to enter because of the crowd. They looked at her curiously, a slim good-looking girl. She found someone who looked to be in command. He spoke to her courteously. As far as he knew, that officer was not here.

The next hotel she went to was similar. And the next. I do not know how many hotels there were in Crewe in wartime. The last one she went to, and it was getting late, the Officer looked kindly at her.

"Young lady," he said, "there are thousands of men in

this town. It is not safe for you to be walking the streets looking for one." She returned to the station at Crewe, desolate. It was late. The next train to Liverpool would be early in the morning. That is why the Crewe railway station still haunts my memory.

She arrived back home and went to bed. I do not think she recovered. He wrote from Paris in 1945. He would be returning soon to the States and would communicate further. In 1947 she booked her ship for Boston and I received permission to marry her in Boston. Before she sailed my mother took ill. The doctor diagnosed a heart attack. My sister cancelled everything and wrote a desperate letter to her fiancée. Later the doctor was proved to have made a wrong diagnosis, but it was too late. Thirty years later on a final visit to Boston, she went into a jeweler's shop to buy something. He, the owner of the business, came to serve her. He looked at her wide-eyed and she to him.

She told me "I knew then that he still loved me, although he had married someone else, and I still loved him. I will never see him again. It would be wrong."

41

Holy Souls
⤚⤙⤚⤙⤚⤙⤚⤙⤚⤙

A few days ago I finished a six days' silent retreat. There is a quality about silence. I find meaningless words more and more irritating, and look for spaces of silence. I threw out the television months ago but still keep a radio, but it looks up at me with an innocent look on its dial as though it knows it is under threat of eviction.

I do not want alien thinkers to put thoughts in my mind, they do not add to my store of wisdom. I want to choose my own sources, for that is the basis of freedom. We are free people; we must value it because the loss of freedom begins in the mind. Without freedom we join the crowd, doing all the same things, frightened of being different, all on the same escalator.

When I was a young student and was sent home from the seminary because I was too ill to continue, I used to look for those silent places, and found them in the open churches. It is difficult to visualise what a loss the open church is to the Catholics of today. They have grown used to the locked church, but it has not enriched their Faith or the Faith of their children or grandchildren. The imagined security of property is less important than the need to grow in Faith and to exercise it in practical ways, one of which is not to give in to fear. Too many words, too much noise, too much fear, they all diminish us and make us less human. It is strange how a silent retreat of only six days can reinforce these convictions. It was helped by the woods, the uplands, the moors and the limestone country, which seem to breathe peace and gentleness everywhere.

There are those who wander across countries and across continents searching for something. They are never very clear what it is. They pick up jobs in various places to support themselves on a temporary basis, and then they pass on, when they say to themselves "it's not here." In my lifetime I have met many of them. They are characterised by their qualities. They are rarely materialistic. They are ready to listen. They give away as much as they take. They are restless to reach a truth and certainty about something beautiful.

This week a man phoned me. He had the kind of accent which made it difficult for me to understand what he was saying. I realised he came from either the Highlands of Scotland or the Glens of Antrim. He had met me at the storytelling sessions on the island of Cape Clear, in the southernmost farmhouse on the edge of the Atlantic. He wanted to meet me and I agreed to meet outside the Shankly Gates of Liverpool football club. There we met. I took him to the Albert Dock, had a meal and talked. We had time and the surroundings were right. He had all the qualities, eager, not materialistic, searching, artistic, musical. I just listened and loved it.

It was the opposite of the rich young man of the Gospel, but the search was the same. We wandered into the Tate and then the Maritime Museum. Then it was time for me to go. I left him outside the Shankly Gates where we had met. And what is all this, except a flight from the world in search of Beauty, Truth, Life? Looking back down the long centuries when Europe was forming, and Asia, China and Africa were already very different, I could see a constant pattern. Anthony of Egypt moving into the desert, Simon

Styletes, St. Benedict at Subiaco, St Bruno, St. Bernard, St. Hilda of Whitby, Hildegard of Bingen, St Benedict Joseph Labre and John Bradburne. They all wandered the world looking for silent places, away from useless words, and noise, from the people on the escalator, silent places where freedom could grow within them.

They have enriched our world. A short time after my retreat I was helping with a Cursillo at the Life Centre. I was aware, in the chapel, of the very special atmosphere which attaches to places that have been prayed in. I realised then that this had been the chapel in which young women had found the courage to give themselves totally to a service of Jesus, which required a vow of chastity, obedience and poverty. It was here that they agonised, searched and found.

42

Do People Really Have Visions Today?

∽∂∽∂∽∂∽∂∽∂∽∂

Recently I was taken to a meal in a restaurant attached to a pub in Croft. Croft is an old village which finds itself the centre of a growing circle of offices and financial buildings on the outskirts of the farmland, all little rivulets of the growing tide of prosperity coming in to Warrington.

But the pub where I was eating had been a blacksmith's establishment at the time of the French Revolution. Big men with hairy chests had been making and fitting horseshoes there in the 1780's, in a village which went back centuries.

When the smithy became a pub they called it The Horseshoe. During all the years of muted persecution of Catholics in England, known to us as "the penal times" when fear and even hatred of Catholicism ran like a hidden tide under the talk of polite company, a French priest fleeing from the French Revolution came to Croft and was accepted. He was accepted because Britain was at war with Napoleon and the people received someone who had suffered under him. In 1827, after Catholic Emancipation, he built the church at Croft. Meanwhile, in the corner of the blacksmith's shop down the lane, a young lad used to curl up and sleep after an exhausting day at the forge.

No one knew where he came from. He was a big lad, still growing, he drifted over the Pennines from Yorkshire looking for work. He was a Catholic. A teenager who could read and write. A homeless teenager looking for work. No big issue, the smithy gave him shelter and enough food to keep the muscles strong.

But this growing lad, who worked long hours of exhausting effort, fasted all through the Lent of 1827. That meant no meat, no eggs, no milk, one meal a day.

Each Sunday he went to Mass at Southworth Hall until the new church opened. In modern England, where there is no persecution of anyone because of religion, he would be far from a normal Catholic teenager.

As Palm Sunday approached, he prepared for Confession, and left the confessional leaping for joy. On Easter Sunday he hurried, once more leaping for joy, as he approached the church, which had now opened for public worship.

During the Mass something happened that was awesome. He saw the figure of Christ standing by the altar with light pouring from Him upon the kneeling boy and a companion who was with him. In one hand He held a globe and the other hand was raised in blessing.

A warm glow flowed through the young apprentice. He lost count of time. On the way out he shyly asked the other lad if he had seen anything unexpected. He was answered by the total silence of the other. Sometime later he drifted back over the Pennines into Yorkshire.

When he was an old man he wrote his account of what happened in dated copperplate writing on four sheets of notepaper, giving intimate details of the event which, he said, affected the whole of his life. The four sheets were found by chance and read for the first time late in the 1900's. It is a wonderful story which raises issues from many different viewpoints.

Do people really have visions like this even in our secular world? They do indeed, but not in the same way.

Most of the spiritual visions are internal rather than external and I have listened to account after account of them over the years, many of them from men, many of them from priests. They are extraordinary accounts of men and women altered dramatically by a religious experience which is unique and overpowering. Genuine scientific researchers into truth do not deny the phenomenon.

But people with faith understand that this is the incursion of the love of God into the lives of men and women who so often seem 'ordinary' to us, but they never look like that to God who loves the inner beauty which we cannot see.

Hard men in prison, girls on the street selling themselves, cooks and plumbers, doctors and dentists, politicians and royals... the list is endless. Sometimes I think that every man and woman worldwide, in every religious or non-religious group, are open to it. Atheists and agnostics can be knocked off their perches just as swiftly as the 'credulous' peasant they once sneered at. He is the Lord who loves and love is a consuming fire. All He wants is "Yes."

43

Links With The Very Poorest
✌ᷓᷢ᷀✌ᷓᷢ᷀✌ᷓᷢ᷀✌ᷓᷢ᷀✌ᷓᷢ᷀

Some years ago, when Liverpool Council was controlled by the Labour Party, the Senior Citizens of Merseyside were given the right to travel free on Merseyside rail and bus services.

It was a generous and rational gesture of goodwill. It should be extended nationwide as it is in the Irish republic. Any casual observer in Lancashire or Greater Manchester can see the difference. Buses and trains in those areas often run almost empty except at times of going to work or returning. No one gains by being miserly.

Generosity is loving and creative. God bless the Councillors who gave us the gift. After years on bikes and being cooped up in cars, it is great to run for a train, step into warm space, hurtle quickly to a destination and know that the little plastic pass in my pocket is all the inspector wants to see. It also re-establishes links with the poor who cannot afford a car.

This is especially true of the buses where chatter is easier and opens up fascinating glimpses into other people's joys and sorrows. The Gospel account of the three years of the life of Jesus, teaching and healing the crowds, is constantly in front of my mind these days.

He gave up home ownership when He left Nazareth and took on a life without material security. That put Him in the midst of the poor and voiceless multitude. Too young to get a bus pass, but the basis from which He gave the teaching and healing power, which still guides and illuminates the world.

This has to be one of the marks which attracts the modern man and woman to the Church, but too often it is missing; they only see the Church as a showpiece of power and privilege.

It is interesting to see the interplay of relationships between the young men and women, the girls and boys who crowd the trains between 3.30pm and 4.30pm. There is a sense of freedom in the way they act and talk and laugh together. There is no suggestion of fear or oppression. This is the generation which seems most firmly to have rejected the Liturgy of the Christian Church whether in the Catholic, Anglican or Protestant manner.

It is difficult for older people, like myself, to dialogue with them. If they are young they have not been able to formulate their views and they follow the crowd. If they are older they become aggressive about what they feel. But there are many who can dialogue with them and it is important to listen.

It has been suggested that the most important act which made an impact on the national consciousness in the past ten years was the production of the Bishops' document entitled "The Common Good," which came out before the general election of 1997.

It was a document about the teaching of the Catholic Church about social justice. The second factor, probably more significant still, has been the growth of CAFOD and its work in the world of the underprivileged. What enhances this is the record of CAFOD working alongside the people of the countries they help, engaging them as partners in their projects. It is this work particularly that calls on the idealism of young people in our schools who have shown their commitment by fasting, fundraising and other activities. They also support environmental subjects and are interested in human rights.

These topics are part of the teaching of the Catholic Church and are rooted deeply in Biblical themes. When I was young (long time ago!) these things were not on our agenda. We stayed with the three-fold division of the catechism The Creed, The Sacraments The Commandments. We also learned prayers and hymns. We had to escape the evil world, mortal sin and hell, the object to get oneself into heaven.

I must admit that when later, in Philosophy, I met with the Young Christian Worker Movement and the contact with the Social Encyclicals, a new and truly exciting world opened up for me.

Maybe we should encourage the young in their search for Justice and Peace, and suggest to them that the cult figure who led and still leads to their ideals is Jesus of Nazareth, who taught that at the end of time we will not be judged on our sacramental life or our sex life but on "I was hungry and you gave me food, I was thirsty and you gave me drink. I was naked and you clothed me. I was sick, in prison and you visited me."

44

The Questionnaire
୭ଡ଼୭ଡ଼୭ଡ଼୭ଡ଼୭ଡ଼

A pair of boots plastered with dried Dubbin and mud, in a plastic bag in the boot of a car, and I was all set for a day in the Lakes. The sun was shining, the hills were green and the mountains had wreathes of mist floating around them. I had two youngish priests with me, and sufficient food and fluids for a day in the hills. We finished with the sunshine floating out of the very bones in our bodies as the evening chill set in. On the way home I dropped in for a meal to Jim and Peggy's. A group of friends had also gathered there. It was one of those golden days.

When I was back in the flat, night had fallen. I opened a letter, which had been pushed through my letterbox. It was from the Doctor's Surgery. It read "We are now offering a yearly check up to all our patients aged 75 or over, so we are writing to find out how you are at the moment." I thought "What a good idea. I should have done this when I was parish priest." I read on.

There was a questionnaire, tick 'yes' or 'no'. Do you live alone? Do you look after anyone? Are there often days when you don't see anyone? Can you usually go out by yourself without someone to help you? Can you walk around inside the house without someone to help you? Are there days when you are unable to prepare a meal for yourself? Is it difficult to get a hot drink when you need one? Do you usually need help to get yourself washed and dressed? Do you usually need help with getting in and out of bed?

I put the letter down on the table. It was a sobering reminder of reality of life for many over 75's. By what kind of law had I been allowed to enjoy a day like today? The thought did not go away. It began to be asked during the prayer time in the early morning. It kept coming back, intruding into sacred space. The rather daft question. 'why does God ...?' and daft indeed, because who but God can fathom the mind of God?

But it kept coming back, demanding answers. It mixed with the vision of the crowds who would be swirling all around me in the Cathedral on Sunday. The people younger than I, and riddled with sickness, infirmity, anxiety, arthritis, cancer, heart trouble, yes indeed, and much younger people dragged into drugs by sneering peer groups when they were too young to say no. Kids led into alcohol and cannabis and then alcoholism and heroin, kids with their childhood cut short and destroyed by 'safe sex.' Saints and sinners reaching out to the Eternal Lover in the afternoon sunlight filtering through the great red, blue, green windows of the majestic circle of the Cathedral. I remembered the last two occasions and the sense of the 'Presence' during the Mass, the Presence of Jesus crucified and risen at the centre of the wounded people of God.

Then the enthronement of the Host and the movement of people around the periphery of the Cathedral where so many looked for the Sacrament of Reconciliation, the crowds surging forward to be prayed over and anointed with the oil of gladness, then kneeling, as they did spontaneously on the marble circle of the sanctuary steps. So! 'Why does God?' seemed to be the wrong question.

The people who came to the Cathedral and who would come again on Sunday did not come for an answer to that question. They came for a deeper need than the answer to a pointless question. They would come for a number of reasons known only to themselves, although healing of spirit or body would be very much in the forefront. I knew also that many would come because of the urging of family or friends to 'just try it'. And yet with all this, the filling in of the simple form from the doctor stirred something in me. Why should I be able to put ticks in the 'no' boxes on this form when so many others could not.

I picked up the Bible and opened it at random. It opened at the story of Naaman the Syrian general who had leprosy. A Jewish slave girl told him to go to Israel and see the prophet Elisha. The prophet told him to bathe seven times in the Jordan. The Syrian was angry and said no. But his servants told him to try it. He was cured immediately. Naaman told the world that the God of Israel was truly God. So our questioning and our anger gets us nowhere. What we do know is that Jesus is the Lord, and that He lives and walks among us.

45

Images Of Loneliness In Mind
❦❧❦❧❦❧❦❧❦❧

I think back to the meetings of the parish council when I was still a parish priest. The inevitable points made at the approach of the Christmas season were usually "What about the poor families? And the lonely people?"

The answer to the poor families was left for the member of the SVP who sat at the table and made notes as we talked. He was a big man who smoked little cigars and a person highly respected in the larger community. He remarked that lonely people were old and living alone in a one-bedroom flat. This judgment, delivered with the solemn weight of years in the Society of St Vincent de Paul, was accepted with a nodding of heads around the table, as though the information itself was putting a hot dinner on all those lonely tables.

I was one of those who nodded. And now, guess what? I am an old person living in a one-bedroom flat! But before you start buying tissues to cope with this sad fact, or ordering a hot dinner from Tesco for December 25, I assure you that I do not suffer from loneliness just yet. But I could do. It tears at the hearts of millions, triggered off in so many different ways: the death of someone you loved, away from home in a place or land where people do not look at you, smile at you, speak to you, a child at a boarding school. These are all classic examples of loneliness produced by life situations.

But the most difficult to understand is the person who carries loneliness at the very centre of their heart. They carry it with them. Changing the place where they live or the country where they live does not heal the condition. It must be very difficult to diagnose the root cause of this loneliness, to see whether it is coming from a rejection in early childhood, or even being a baby who was a "mistake" and resented even in the womb, but allowed to live. For in a unique way the condition of inner loneliness comes from a separation from love.

Love is at the very root of life. The author of life is God and God is Love. If love is missing from the very beginning of life the harm done can be very deep, even though the growing person is given all the amenities and sops of our secular society... toys and teddy bears, sweets and treats are just stored garbage if love is missing.

At the very centre of the Christmas story is the pregnancy of Mary, the sensitivity of St Joseph and the birth of a baby. One of the core factors of this mystery of the Word made Flesh is that the two people asked to co-operate were a couple who loved each other deeply, a young man and young woman.

Mary had been chosen and prepared before her birth by the gift of Divine life and the indwelling of the Holy Spirit. She carried within her the history of her nation and the burning longing for the Saviour, the Messiah, so her love for the unborn babe was immeasurably heightened by the glimpse into mystery contained in the message of the angel Gabriel.

St Joseph had not been prepared in the same way, but his simple faith was heroic. His assent was masculine, it was shot through with courage of a high order. He was a big man.

You can see the lessons are striking and relevant to life in our society. There are many good things in the society that has been created in our country over the past years: all this striving for equality, lifting up the poor of our land, giving education to our immigrants and striving to make a person's colour no barrier but an advantage, above all the provision of free health care in a way that could not have been dreamed of in previous centuries. It is a magnificent achievement by the men and women of our day.

But there is a fatal flaw at the heart of our society. When clerks in offices across the country can send out forms where there is no mention of husband and wife, but just "your partner" they indicate a sickness of mammoth proportions. They are saying that a lifelong commitment to love is missing.

One Christmas Day some years ago I had promised to bring Holy Communion to an old woman in a flat who was unable to come to Mass. She was alone; a gas fire burning low gave little warmth. She had a white cloth on a table and a candle lit. On the mantlepiece there was a solitary Christmas card. It had been sent by the Legion of Mary. Only Jesus had broken into her solitude. It was all she wanted, but the images have stayed in my mind.

46

The Wreath
✎🔊✎🔊✎🔊✎🔊✎🔊

Advent is a blessed time; even the secular world gets ready for the birthday of Jesus. The shops all glowing with coloured lights and tinsel, the Christmas trees in town centres, the singing of carols, buskers in the streets, excitement in the faces of children, the office parties. There is nothing religious about it, apparently.

When I was a parish priest I used to feel frustrated by that very conviction. The pre-Christmas celebrations brought lots of creamy profit to the fat cats of industry, but very little to the salvation of souls. But I did find it useful. And it's about this I want to write.

First Communion groups were not easy to handle. The parents of first communicants were willing to come to a few meetings, but most of them had no close connection with the liturgy of Sunday before or after the peak point of the first communion day. I felt I needed to see each family's parents individually. So, with the cooperation of the head teacher of the infant school who sent out the notices, I arranged to see them in fifteen-minute intervals starting at 9.15am to 3pm, during the number of days needed to see them. The Head allowed me to use a spare room in the school for the purpose.

The response of the parents was astonishing. Men and women got permission to leave work in factory or office if necessary, and their employers accepted that as a "one-off." It was a reasonable request. Some parents wrote in to say it was not possible, but they did apologise. It was exhausting for me, but worthwhile. All the parents were concerned about the Faith of their children, but their difficulties were great. They were poorly paid. They had mortgages to pay and could not risk losing their jobs which required hours that normally made Mass difficult for them. Also, there were pleas by their children to join football teams or dancing classes and so on.

By this time, in my old age, I had realised that if I could help them to Christianise their homes, the weekly Mass would inevitably follow. I opened this up to them as a priority and told them some of the practices in their domestic life which they should follow. These things they promised to do. For Advent, I requested the use of the advent wreath That would involve taking the children into the countryside to gather the materials, holly, ivy, twigs and so on, then the making of the wreath in the home with the children helping, then the buying of the red candles.

I gave them a prayer to be said while lighting the candles, one each week, the prayer to be said and the candle lit shortly before the children went to bed. Then the completion of the task by being with the children at one of the Christmas Masses. All this they promised to do. I would give them a similar task in Lent. I also made clear that the reception of First Communion was not conditional on all this happening.

That pressure is unfair - I said so. In the course of the next weeks leading up to Christmas I had occasionally to call in and see people to fix up various things, and inevitably one or two of the homes were the homes of the new advent wreaths. They would show me in proudly and take me to see the masterpiece.

It was in one of these chance visits that I met with the Solicitor. I don't know how he got the name. He had worked at the docks for some years. When I asked one of his mates he said it was because he was always standing at the bar.

The name had stuck and had been abbreviated to Solly. He had left the docks and now was working in a factory. He had the nose of a drinker and had put on weight. The wreath was there, on a small table. He told me that his wife worked in a pub in the evenings and he had the job of seeing the children to bed. He loved his children and the saying of the prayer was his responsibility. "How about the Mass?" I said. He looked at me. "To tell you the truth Father," he said, "I have a problem. The big girl has told me that her mates have heard about the wreath and the prayer, and she is scared because they skit her. I don't want to cause her trouble." "Thanks for telling me, Solly," I said," I understand" But truly I did not understand, nor do I now. But I have never loved a daughter and had to look inside her mind to see its fear.

47

Contemplating The Miracles Of Lourdes And The Miracles That Go Unheralded

෯෯෯෯෯෯෯෯෯෯

I did not expect, in Lourdes, to be involved with one of the inspirational modern movements which has sprung up in the post-Vatican II era.

I must confess to my shame that I went there to try to get away from new movements, to hunt out some of the old fashioned devotions which have survived over the years and still mean such a lot.

However, when our group met on the first evening of the flight, when we had claimed our rooms and sat around after eating the evening meal, I asked what they thought we should see. They made the usual suggestions, the Grotto, the Cachot, the basilicas, etc. One of the group said "The Coenaculo." "What is that?" they all asked. He explained then the epic story of an Italian nun who had opened, in various countries, a number of communities formed of drug addicts who had determined to find a new existence clean of drugs and hopelessness. Two such communities, he explained, were on the outskirts of Lourdes. I agreed to go with him, when I was free to do so, which happened to be three days later when the sun was slowing everything down, except the cars and coaches which threatened the lives of the pilgrims on their way to pray at the Grotto. A woman, Paula, joined us. She knew Bernard, she had introduced him to the Coenaculo at Medugorje.

We passed a beggar at the side of the road. I felt in my pocket for a euro, but Paula stopped me, went over to the man and, offered him a picture of the Divine Mercy, pointed to the prayer on the back and whispered words of encouragement to him. Then, as we moved on, she said to me: "You should not give them money, it feeds their weakness, but give them food if they want it, and above all talk with them and offer them a prayer." This was her way and she assured me it worked.

We made our way up a steep pathway, which was once the route taken by St Bernadette when she travelled from Bartres to Lourdes. The path became a narrow one leading up into the lower slopes of the Pyrenees. There in a lovely valley was the men's Coenaculo. Four years ago it was a derelict barn. The young men had re-roofed it, put in electricity, cleared the land and planted vegetables. They had built a dormitory in a separate building and a refectory. They were also building a chapel of austere beauty which was nearly complete.

We were made welcome. They knew Paula. On this occasion she had sponsored two victims of heroin and cocaine whom she had found on the streets of London and begged the Lourdes communities to take them so that they might begin to live again.

There are twenty-five young men in this community. They have no money and no funding. The food they eat is given to them almost daily by well-wishers. Otherwise they go hungry. They rise at six o'clock to have an hour of prayer and the rosary.

After a hot drink and some bread they go out to work on the building and the farm. More prayer at midday. After a light lunch and a rest they go out once more to work. After the evening meal they spend a further length of time in prayer and then retire. There is no radio or television and no newspapers. Every victim of drugs admitted to the community is given a "Guardian Angel", a mature member of the community who stays with the newcomer night and day until the young man or woman (in the female community) is through the first tortured days of coming off the drugs.

Once integrated into a community, young men and women find a sense of exhilarating freedom the like of which they have not had even in their years of innocence. They freely agree to give part of their life to helping others who are victims of the drug trade.

A deep bond of Christian love develops in each community. It finds expression in the joy which is apparent, and in the services they render to each other.

The very buildings and the opening up of agricultural work they do is reminiscent of the civilising influence of the monasteries of the Middle Ages in Europe. That night, at the Grotto, in the darkness surrounded by whispering pilgrims from many countries, I meditated on the miracle of Lourdes and the stories of spiritual miracles which have not yet been told and maybe never will.

48

Michele

࿇࿇࿇࿇࿇࿇࿇࿇࿇࿇࿇

Early in the morning, long before dawn on the morning of 6th December, Michele slipped out of this world, held in the arms of her mother with the family standing around her bed praying for her eternal peace. The long agony was over, it was time for resurrection. As the Gospel of St. Luke reads "on the first day of the week, at the first sign of dawn the women went to the tomb, but the stone had been rolled away and the body of Jesus was not there." And the message of the angels was "He is not here, He is risen."

The extraordinary vision of Faith tells us that Michele was not there, she was risen. Yes, her body is still with us, shrouded now in wood awaiting its own resurrection when the fullness of time has come. But the dynamic personality whom we call Michele has gone to Jesus, of whom St. Paul in the letter to the Romans wrote, "Neither death, not life, no angel, no prince, nothing that exists, nothing still to come not any power or height or depth can ever come between us and love of God made visible in Christ Jesus our Lord." She was born in 1958 on the twenty first of November, the eldest of the two children of Jim and Mary Hampson. Her brother Peter was born soon after. From the beginning it was a family with deep and unbreakable love for each other, a love which reached out to any in the community who were in need

The love was strengthened by a deep religious Faith that never wavered in all the storms of life, but particularly it has up held them in this moment of deep sadness. Baptised at St. Bartholomew's Michele Mary, her infant school days followed and her first communion, then Junior school, St. Mary's here in Birchley. She finished her formal education at Carmel College and opted to begin her working career as an assistant in a post office. Soon after she married and Elizabeth was born. She bought the rights to a small sub post office and it flourished. But her marriage did not. She found herself a single mother with a young child. She sold the sub post office and began a meteoric career in post offices in greater Merseyside and was appointed senior area manager.

Early in her forty-first year, the first signs of the cancer began to show itself. It was a virulent, fast growing attack. It was at this time that I began to see her with regularity and she came to our healing services. Her spiritual growth was faster than any attack on her physical frame. She prayed, never gave up hope, talked to all of the effect of prayer on her life. She came under the care of a Consultant who became also a very major part of her battle to regain her health. He and his colleagues supported her with all the resources of science and the power of the NHS.

Her admiration for these doctors, especially her own consultant, was unbounded and she told the story of their devotion to all and sundry. Three times over these years it seemed as though the combination of spiritual help and the resources of science would eliminate the growth. But the re-emergence for the fourth time was too much. All through these years her love of life and her dynamism was undiminished. She took Elizabeth to Florida, Majorca, Lourdes. She raised thousands of pounds for cancer research. She organised and worked with friends and inspired them. She talked faith hope and charity to the sick people she came in contact with. She was being stripped of everything. Her love for God increased with each setback. Finally the only tie binding her strongly to this world was her love for Elizabeth and for Jim, Mary and Peter. Some four weeks ago when I saw her she said, "I've had enough. I am longing to see the face of Christ and the face of Our Lady. All I want is to go to heaven."

It was nearly time for her to go. She left all the instructions for her funeral this morning and other explicit instructions in family matters, then typical of Michele she asked her brother Peter to take her to London and let her ride on the big wheel. He took her and her wheel chair to London, she rode on the big wheel, spent money on a good meal, stayed at the Hilton Hotel. Seven days later the Bridegroom came for her. "See where He stands behind our wall, He looks in at the window, He peers through the lattice. He says to me 'Come then my love for see the winter is past, the rains are over and gone, the flowers appear on the earth the season of glad songs has come. Come then my love, my lovely one, come. Let me hear your voice, for your voice is sweet and your face is beautiful' ." Eternal rest give to her O Lord.

49

The Christmas Spirit
࿆ఞ࿆ఞ࿆ఞ࿆ఞ࿆ఞ࿆ఞ

I knew we were getting near to the 'Season of goodwill' when a young adolescent, possibly fourteen years old, courteously offered me a seat on an overcrowded train. Later, in the same journey, a young girl towering over me straightened my rain hood so that it fitted over my head, and smiled at me as she did so. On a train to Leeds, a group of Asians playing cards on an adjoining table on the train approached me and asked with the greatest courtesy if I could take an empty seat so that a fourth card player could join them. This, of course, was to their advantage, but it was their polite manner that struck me.

"What's happening?" I said to myself, used as I am to a different kind of culture. "Is it because it is Christmas? Or is a new world emerging?" But on devoting more time to thinking about it, I came to the realisation that I look like a little old man and, in fact, I am one. So perhaps as I get older still the inborn sense of pity for the helpless which is in the background of so much of the Christian instinct to do good works will eventually cocoon me. Nor do I wish to leave Jews and Muslims and Sikhs out of it, nor even the curious atheists and agnostics who come forward and top up the money when we run garden parties and Christmas Fairs to raise a certain sum for something which appeals to their sense of fair play. I am sure they do much more while still feeling distaste for religion. But the best was still to come.

The Trans Pennine Express, which is the optimistic name they give to the rail journey, is sometimes an uncertain express. Of course the train rattles through various tunnels on its way through the Pennines, going in and out of them like a rabbit shopping for Christmas, so I guess there are excuses, but this day it was right on time pulling into Sunderland. There are two exits from the station. The nuns waiting for me went to the main exit. I had no idea that there were two exits and left by a kind of back door. Outside was a taxi. It was a big vehicle. I felt lonely inside it. The driver was not English but he talked with a Geordie accent. I told him the street I wanted and that it was a convent and that it was a very large school in the recent past. He said, "Yes. I know that." But he didn't.

We wandered around Sunderland as I anxiously watched the clock knocking up the cash, stopped at a convent which I knew was the wrong one, but went inside with my driver to confront a man with a florid face behind an official table with telephones and files on it. "No," he said, it was not the right one. Did he know where the other was? "No" he said, he lived somewhere out in the country. In modern England they always live somewhere else, but he spoke English. And that was a help.

So the taxi and the 'fare' went on the road again with the fare looking at the clock and wondering if maybe a credit card might help. But eventually we arrived at the convent. He stepped out, opened my door, handed me my rucksack. I reached in my pocket. "No," he said, "that will be alright."

There was a full moon in the sky, the air was frosty. In a neighbouring street a busker was playing "God rest you merry gentlemen, may nothing you dismay." A picture of his hungry wife and children flashed into my mind. "You can't do that," I said, "it's your livelihood." He smiled down at me, stepped into the taxi. "Say a prayer for me," he said and drove off into the night. In the convent, peace was all pervasive, and when, in the early morning, I heard them singing "Hear the herald voice resounding 'Christ is near', it seems to say 'I cast away the dreams of darkness to welcome Christ, the light of day.'" I knew it was still Advent, but the wonder of Christmas casts its light forward and I guess some part of it had fallen upon me. Possibly I look for the good things and ignore the sour ones, and that makes a difference. So next Tuesday four of my friends are taking me to see Scrooge. They suggest it might help.

Wishes for Christmas
These are my wishes for Christmas.
That fighting may cease everywhere.
That the rich may invite someone needy
To 'come in and pull up a chair.'
That all children receive, in their stocking,
The shelter and peace of a home.
Where everyone's gentle and kindly
And nobody's left on their own.
When friendship abounds in the pleasure
Of finding a gift that's just right
And everyone celebrates Christmas,
The day and the most Holy Night.
When parishioners gather together,
In a church full of love and of peace.
These are my wishes for Christmas
With the hope that these joys never cease.

P. Williams

50

Only God Reads The Depths Of The Human Spirit
ళ్యాళ్యాళ్యాళ్యాళ్యాళ్య

I think it was just before Christmas that two events nearly coincided. One was the capture of Saddam Hussein, the other was the conviction of a youngish man named Ian Huntley.

The interest in Saddam Hussein, and the anger my friends showed at the memory of his past misdeeds, soon faded away. Huntley seemed endlessly to occupy the news carriers. "The Headline," which editors of various tabloids tell us is the chief item of world news worth knowing, featured Huntley until he had been analysed, the police censured, and the e-mail writers found something else to whinge about. It all happened in that happy season in which the music floating on the frosty air was Jingle Bells, Rudolph the Red Nosed Reindeer and other classics of a buried age.

Saddam had murdered, tortured his way to power, and then been guilty of crimes against humanity making him a suspect of war crimes and terrorism on a cosmic scale. Huntley had murdered two little girls. Some of my female friends said they were praying for "poor Saddam Hussein". How true it is that only the Spirit of God, who alone knows the depths of God as St. Paul wrote in the Letter to the Romans, knows the depths also of the human spirit. Judgments are rarely wise and rarely based on mere reason. We don't live like that.

A few days ago a young gentleman of my acquaintance wished to meet a young lady whom I also knew. He made an appointment to meet. He was very late. She was walking up and down a cold and foggy street and went to a public phone box to phone him. Because she was short of change and short of time, she put in a new shiny pound coin. No answer from the other side. She pressed the button to get her coin back. But no coin fell into her hand. After two more attempts she gave up and went back to her car and decided to drive up and down a circle of streets to see if she could find him. Meanwhile the young gentleman had gone to the same phone box to phone her. Again he got no answer. He pressed the button. No money dropped. He looked at the instrument closely and noticed an obstacle blocking the mechanism. He prised it away and a shower of money fell into his hands. He took the money and walked away. His mother had given him a Christmas present, a pair of new gloves. He left them in the phone box in his jubilation at the pennies from heaven.

Walking up and down the street in hope of seeing the lady, he saw a dishevelled gentleman enter the phone box, press the useless button and leave. "I wonder," he thought, "was he the manipulator?" Meanwhile the lady saw him and took him into the car. As they drove down the street, he saw the shrunken figure of the man in the phone box, walking in the crowds. "Stop the car," he said. He leapt out and ran across the street dodging the traffic. He stopped the man, pressed all the money into his hands. The man looked at him, his eyes full of tears of gratitude. He said something in a foreign tongue, and then, haltingly, 'thank you.' He reached into his pocket and took out a pair of gloves and pressed them into the hands of his benefactor. They were the gloves his mother had given him. It was then he realised that he had lost them. They parted. The stranger was lost in the crowd. My acquaintance crossed the busy road to the car.

The brief encounter was over. The lady questioned him when she drove away with him "What was all that about?" she said.... He told her the story. "I knew he was very poor, as soon as I saw him. The money I took was all he had to hope for." And yet on such trifling incidents did St. Francis of Assisi begin his pathway to heaven, which altered the Church of God in the middle ages and left a golden legend for all time.

The way we see our world is not always the way God sees it. And so, to come back to Saddam Hussein, in a short account of his life the historian told of a childhood of brutality and beatings inflicted on a young child whose name was Saddam by a father who did not love him, The child left home for the streets of the big cities. That also was just an insignificant item of news which would never have dominated any newspaper. But we have to beware. Only the Spirit of God reads the depths of the human spirit.

Shadows

Shadows

Shadows

Shadows